GRAHAM PHYTHIAN

SOUTH
MANCHESTER
Remembered

GRAHAM PHYTHIAN

SOUTH MANCHESTER

Remembered

The
History
Press

First published 2012

The History Press
The Mill, Brimscombe Port
Stroud, Gloucestershire, GL5 2QG
www.thehistorypress.co.uk

British Library Cataloguing in Publication Data.
A catalogue record for this book is available from the British Library.

ISBN 978 0 7524 7002 3

Typesetting and origination by The History Press
Printed in Great Britain
Manufacturing managed by Jellyfish Print Solutions Ltd

CONTENTS

ACKNOWLEDGEMENTS

My thanks to the following for supplying information, material, and amendments and additions to the original articles: David Barrow, Phil Blinston, Neil Bonner, Sue Boothby, Ida Bradshaw, Duncan Broady, John Clarke, Peter Cooper, June Cowan, Jill Cronin, Kate Dibble, Brian Donat, Norman P. Duck, Rev. Greg Forster, Abdul Ghaffar, Edward Gray, David Hall, Rob Hall, Jane Hardwick, K.C. Hawker, David Hodgkins, Diane Inglis, Dave Kierman, Bernard Leach, Chris Lee, Diana Leitch, Philip Lloyd, Steve McDonald, Ian McIlvanney, Janet Phillips, Abdul Qayyum, Brian R. Robinson, Andy Simpson, Ian Stewart, Anne Tucker, George Turnbull, Eric Watson, Jon West, Colin Wilkinson, Prue Williams, Roy Young.

Also the staff of the following libraries: Manchester Central, Chorlton, Didsbury, Withington, Levenshulme, and Sale.

Additionally, the staff of Greater Manchester Police Museum and Archives, Greater Manchester Museum of Transport, Manchester Southern Cemetery, Levenshulme Antiques and Crafts Village, and the Manchester Museum.

My thanks also go to members of Chorlton Local History Society, Friends of Platt Fields, Friends of Victoria Baths, and Didsbury, Withington and Northenden Civic Societies.

Every reasonable effort has been made to trace the copyright owners of the visuals used herein. Any omission or oversight should be sent in writing to the author c/o The History Press.

INTRODUCTION

This is by no means a complete picture of the history of South Manchester. Churches, suffragettes, and the University get nary a mention, and (for example) the great theatrical tradition of Didsbury's Athenaeum is celebrated elsewhere. Buildings are in here only if there's a good story attached to them. I'm sure the reader will be aware of other omissions which s/he feels should be rectified.

By way of explanation, if not excuse, allow me to tell you how this book came about.

A couple of years ago the *South Manchester Reporter* was looking for someone to examine the claim that You'll Never Walk Alone was first sung by a football crowd at Old Trafford by members of Chorlton-cum-Hardy Operatic Society in around 1960. As a soccer historian who lived locally, I entered the newspaper's radar, so I was asked to do some digging. The very interesting outcome of that particular piece of research may be found in the section entitled 'On a Carousel' (see page 68).

The Reporter must have liked the results, as I was then asked to write a weekly column on local history. Originally intended to last just twelve weeks, at the time of writing it's been going strong for two and a half years – even allowing for the fact that I now alternate with Diana Leitch, who took over in 2010 when I was snowed under with other duties. This book is a collection of my contributions, suitably updated and amended.

I was glad to receive a couple of corrections early on, as this meant people were actually reading the column! It also meant that my research had to be spot-on. The people who took the time to comment or put me right are gratefully included in the acknowledgements.

I hope that there's enough in these pages to instruct, intrigue or even entertain. If any of your own memories are triggered by the book's contents, do get in touch with me c/o the *South Manchester Reporter*. We may even be able to fill in those gaps!

Graham Phythian, 2012

PRE-DECIMAL CURRENCY CONVERTER

1 guinea = £1.05p

Half a crown (2s 6d) = 12½p

1 shilling (1s) = 5p

6 old pence (6d) = 2½p

1 farthing = approximately 0.1p

ONE

GETTING AROUND

OMNIBUS WARS

It's a fairly safe bet that the world's first horse-drawn public omnibus service ran between Manchester and Pendleton in 1824. It was soon followed by others, including the 'country route' south to Rusholme village.

The industry enjoyed rapid growth. By mid-century, Yorkshire entrepreneur John Greenwood kept over 170 horses in his Longsight stables and was deploying a fleet of sixty-four omnibuses all over the city. The service was less copious in the south, but it still reached as far as Plymouth Grove, Victoria Park, and Didsbury.

The three-horse carriage imported by Greenwood from Edinburgh had a new design: by arranging the benches on the exposed top deck so that passengers were seated around the rim facing outwards, more people could be fitted into the space available. The only drawback, until a later model introduced an elevated roof, was that the middle-classes in the more expensive, sheltered, downstairs seats would often have their window view obscured by the dangling lower limbs of the great unwashed.

The lucrative Cheadle–Manchester service brought Greenwood's City Carriage Company into competition with the Cheadle Omnibus Company. For many years, the villages and farms on the route witnessed the spectacle of two early morning buses chock with top-hatted businessmen racing each other north into the city. The Cheadle coach – blue as opposed to Manchester red – added to the razzamatazz by equipping the guard with a bugle, which he sounded to announce their progress along the country roads.

Despite police intervention, the races continued until Greenwood's company bought out their rivals for £800. The deal was supervised by the ubiquitous Fletcher Moss, who had his own omnibus carriage and horses, from which he made a substantial income. He then astutely sold the lot on the coming of the suburban railways.

In the city centre, competition between omnibus services grew fiercer. Anybody who had the wherewithal to look after some horses and maintain a carriage, and either drove or could afford to pay a driver, was able to tout for passengers. As a result, rival companies clashed – sometimes literally – in their battle for custom.

Manchester's internationally celebrated Art Treasures Exhibition at Old Trafford in 1857 (see page 94) acted as a catalyst for more omnibus feuds. Over a thousand passengers per day travelled out to the Exhibition from Market Street, and Greenwood's buses were the most successful, conveying a staggering 1,265,000 paying travellers during the six months. Nonetheless, two other companies did well enough to stay in business after the demand subsided.

The struggle for supremacy took many forms. There was a price war: the City Company operated

Greenwood's Manchester Carriage Company on the Didsbury-Market Street bus-run, *c.* 1860. The building in the background was the Wellington Inn, now Zizzi's Italian restaurant (2011). (Greater Manchester Transport Museum)

a minimax system of 3 pence (1½p) downstairs and 2 pence (1p) on the top deck. Greenwood hit on the idea of delivering late evening post into the city centre, so as to catch the 10 p.m. London mail train. A speed challenge was thrown down, which resulted in a race the length of Market Street between three carriages, one from each of the competing companies. Given the huge crowds that turned out to watch (and no doubt place a few bets), the authorities were powerless to stop the race, despite the fact that serious police warnings had been made public.

The competition only got livelier. There were complaints from the public about 'overcharging, over-loading, and dangerous racing'. Whenever an individual tried to operate on a company's patch, the larger outfit would deploy a bus or two, either to precede the newcomer so as to prevent him taking any passengers, or to crowd the rival to one side of the road, not allowing him to stop. This practice was given the ironic title of 'nursing'.

Injuries to passengers, the bad publicity of court cases, and ample fines, did little to stop the free market becoming a free-for-all. It was only when the arrival of the horse-drawn trams and local trains brought about the demise of the omnibuses that Manchester public transport's brief flirtation with the Wild West came to an end.

FULL CIRCLE?

Here's a question for trivia buffs: what's the connection between the following buildings or facilities in South Manchester?

Morrison's supermarket on Wilbraham Road, Chorlton.

Remedy bar (formerly XS Malarkey's – next door to Sainsbury's) on Wilmslow Road, Fallowfield.

Brankgate private houses, off Lapwing Lane, West Didsbury.

The Tropical Marine Centre on Harper Road (off Longley Lane), Northenden.

The service station at the corner of Mauldeth Road West and Alexandra Road South, Withington.

The Café Rouge bistro opposite Didsbury Library.

The answer is that they are all on the site of, or very close to, defunct railway stations. Before the Beeching Axe notoriously did away with branch lines in the 1960s, there was a network of passenger tracks across South Manchester. From Chorlton Junction (just east of where the new metro-link stop is on St Werburgh's Road) the line from central Manchester split. The south-east branch headed alongside what is now the Nell Lane estate for Withington and Didsbury, en route for Stockport. The eastern track followed Mauldeth Road West to Fallowfield and Levenshulme (South), and then to Guide Bridge.

A steam train at Northenden Station in the 1950s.

This stretch now forms part of the Manchester Cycleway. A third line, further south, which linked Timperley in the west and present-day Tameside in the east, served Northenden.

The *Manchester City News* for Saturday, 3 February 1866, carried an enthusiastic report on the opening of the Northenden line (the only one in the area still in use today). However, not all responses to the new railways were positive. When the Chorlton-Didsbury-Stockport line opened fourteen years later, 'Disgruntled of Withington' – or the Victorian equivalent – had his or her two-penn'orth:

If the Midland Company expect the support of the Withington people on this line, they will have to drop their fares. Five pence for a third class single, and eight pence for a first class single, is too much from Manchester to Withington. Besides this, anyone living near to the village will have a mile to walk from the station.

(From a letter to the *Manchester Guardian*, 5 January 1880)

The visible memories that remain from that steam-powered age are few and far between. There's the clock tower close to the corner of Barlow

The Fallowfield Station sign on Wilmslow Road still exists today. (Graham Phythian)

Moor Road and Wilmslow Road, near Didsbury Library. On Lapwing Lane there's the Railway pub, and on the corner of Burton Lane there was the Midland (named after the railway company), now called the Metropolitan. Further down from the Midland, the walls and cobbles of the approach to Withington station are still there. The disused signal box for the Northenden Junction is still standing by the Longley Lane Bridge. The Remedy bar (at the time of writing the building is currently unoccupied) has the original 'FALLOWFIELD STATION' engraved in stone on an outside wall. Some hefty stone blocks lurking in the undergrowth on the south side of the cycleway, opposite the end of Athol Road, Withington, are remains of the Alexandra Park station platform.

Now that the metro-link branch to Chorlton is up and running, it's perhaps one of the ironies of history that some of the old lines, disused and neglected for so long (apart from the well-maintained Sustrans cycle track), are being resurrected for public transport in the twenty-first century.

TWO

SILVER SCREEN

WITHINGTON'S OSCAR WINNER

A nervous asthmatic lad who stammered, had a pronounced Mancunian accent, and who, according to a former teacher at Central Grammar School, had 'no particular acting talent', seems an unlikely candidate for film stardom. Yet Withington-born Robert Donat, youngest in a family of four boys, rose through the ranks of provincial repertory theatre to the West End stage, launching his Oscar-winning cinema career in 1932 at the age of 27.

It was as a child at the Rusholme Repertory Theatre that he heard a stirring recitation of Dickens' *A Christmas Carol*. Immediately smitten, he set about learning long passages of Shakespeare, which he would recite with gusto at school concerts. The elocutionist James Bernard had helped him standardise his accent and overcome his stammer, and one of Robert's tricks was to shout out dramatic monologues whilst walking down Wilmslow Road, where the noise of the passing trams covered his voice and helped cure him of any self-consciousness.

He was also a frequent patron of Withington's Scala cinema, later renamed Cine City.

Local blacksmith Sam Priday recalled the young Donat's visits to his forge, where they would stage mock fights with real swords. (The concept of health and safety had yet to be formalised, it seems.) The practice must have stood him in good stead for his first lead movie role, that of the Count of Monte Cristo. Now sporting a rakish moustache à la Clark Gable, Donat showed he could swashbuckle with the best of them, inspiring a teenage crush in Judy Garland. To co-opt a cliché, the camera loved him too, this handsome blade with the upper crust English accent and Shakespearean tones.

Alfred Hitchcock chose Donat to play Richard Hannay in the 1935 version of *The 39 Steps*, in which the actor out-suaves Kenneth More and Robert Powell, who took the role in later, less gripping versions. An Oscar nomination for his role in *The Citadel* was followed by an Academy Award for lead actor in *Goodbye Mr Chips* in 1939. It was by no means a shoo-in: he was up against Lawrence Olivier in *Rebecca*, and Clark Gable in the award-festooned blockbuster *Gone With The Wind*. Hollywood for once chose to reward underplaying a role (and that tearjerker of an ending no doubt helped).

Robert Donat won Best Actor Academy Award in 1939 for *Goodbye Mr Chips*.

Donat later said that he had based the part of Mr Chips on his former history teacher at Central Grammar School, a Mr Birkby.

Despite making it into the bigtime, Donat never lost touch with his South Manchester roots. He once said that the three temptations of his life were: 'the White Lion, the Red Lion, and the Golden Lion'. Alas, only one of those three Withington pubs is still standing today.

Equally, Donat remained grateful to those who had helped him in the early years. He last visited Central Grammar School in 1938, when he gave a talk to the pupils, emphasising the debt he owed to the school and its teachers.

The actor died in June 1958, not, as was first thought, from asthma complications, but from a brain tumour.

On 15 May 2011, the long campaign for a permanent local memorial to Robert Donat at last came to fruition, when a commemorative plaque was unveiled by his son, Brian, at 42 Everett Road, Withington.

MANCUNIAN FILMS

Many people in South Manchester know that the early years of BBC TV's *Top of the Pops* were recorded in an old church building on Dickenson Road, Rusholme. Unless you're a cinema buff, you may not be aware that before that it had been a prolific film studio as well.

The owner was John E. Blakeley, whose father, John Snr, had launched Mancunian Films thirty years earlier with a Charlie Chaplin short.

The company, which was to feature George Formby, Tessie O'Shea and top comic Frank Randle, was, however, originally based in London. It had been John Snr's dream to make the films in Manchester, and when the abandoned Rusholme Wesleyan Church building became available in 1947, he considered his £70,000 well spent.

The first Rusholme production, *Cup-Tie Honeymoon*, was a typical Mancunian Films musical comedy. Some sample dialogue:

'Do you believe in love at first sight?'
'Well it certainly saves a lot of time.'

The interiors were filmed in the new studio, and the football scenes at nearby Maine Road. There were early cameos by Pat Phoenix (Coronation Street's Elsie Tanner) and Bernard Youens (Stan Ogden in the same soap), and Jimmy Clitheroe made his film debut here. Extras were found in the nearby Welcome pub, and they were easily persuaded to lend their presence for 'a pie and a pint'.

The energetic, panto-style productions – 'comedy burlesques' – were lapped up by the Manchester audiences, just what the doctor ordered as an antidote to those grim postwar years. Mancunian Films were bigger box office hits in the city than contemporary Hollywood films. The critics, however, were less than impressed. Jimmy Clitheroe is, after all, an acquired taste.

Blakeley continued to give the people what they wanted, turning out a dozen comedies in the next five years. Frank Randle, the highest-paid comic in the country at the time, was a staple, much as Kenneth Williams would be in the *Carry On* saga.

Even Randle must have caught his breath when he realised who was to play opposite him in the final Dickenson Road production *It's a Grand Life* in 1953. His co-star was the 22-year-old peroxide peach Diana Dors. Rumour had it that la Dors had been sent to the cold north as a slap on the wrist for some misdemeanour at Rank studios. Rumour also had it (she was that sort of girl) that she soon grew weary of Randle's off-screen attentions. Well, you can hardly blame the old trouper.

The Dickenson Road studio was sold to the BBC in 1954, and Mancunian Films went back to London. The church is now demolished, but the

Diana Dors and Frank Randle in the Mancunian film *It's a Grand Life*. (C.P. Lee)

film and TV connections are commemorated by the heritage plaque on the wall opposite what is now a cycle shop.

Sadly, when I popped round to the Welcome pub recently, it seemed to be closed. Does any reader have memories of performing as an extra for Mancunian Films?

FUN IN '59

In November 1959, what amusements were available to a South Manchester resident?

No computers, iPods, Wiis, or other sundry quick fixes. There were only two TV channels – BBC and ITV Granada. Highlights for a weeknight's viewing might include Hancock's Half-Hour, the Charlie Drake Show, Wagon Train, and a ruggedly handsome young newcomer by the name of Clint Eastwood in Rawhide. Midweek sport might show amateur boxing or Rugby League.

So, if you could afford it, going out was a powerfully tempting alternative. There were around a dozen cinemas in South Manchester in 1959. Chorlton, Withington, Levenshulme and Northenden each had two, and Fallowfield, Didsbury, Whalley Range and Brooks Bar had one apiece. There was a wide choice of films. At the Tudor in Didsbury you could thrill to Mario Lanza in *For the First Time*, 'filmed in colour in the Mediterranean'. You had all of two weeks in which to catch Charlton Heston taking the tablets in *The Ten Commandments* at the Chorlton Essoldo. You could see one of the all-time best film comedies *Some Like it Hot*, with a rare 'A' certificate, at Fallowfield's Cresta. Levenshulme patrons had possibly the widest choice: *The Inn of the Sixth Happiness* at the Palace, whilst just down Stockport Road at the ABC Regal, entertainment was provided by *Jack the Ripper*.

Withington's Scala, later Cine City, has recently been demolished. A few of the old cinema buildings are still standing, but with a different function. The Savoy, later renamed the Gaumont, in Chorlton, is now a Co-op funeral parlour. Further down Barlow Moor Road, the one-time Essoldo has been demolished, with a fast food bar now on the site. The Levenshulme Palace was turned into a nightclub, and is now a restaurant. In Northenden, my own favourite cinema haunt, the ABC Forum, has long since been transformed into a Jehovah's Witness Assembly Hall. The old ABC 'fan' logo atop the centre of the building's façade has been incorporated into the new design.

I have many fond memories of that cinema, besides the many great films I saw there. The usherette's flashlight prowling the back row for any untoward canoodling. The rhythmical stomping on the wooden floorboards during the film's boring

The Essoldo cinema on Barlow Moor Road, Chorlton. Today, a take-away occupies the site. (Manchester Central Library Local Image Collection: ref.m09200)

bits, guaranteed to drive the same poor usherette to apoplexy. The (usually unsuccessful) attempt to hide beneath the seats after a performance, so as to see the film again for free.

There were other places worth going, of course. The Levenshulme Palais de Danse advertised 'Continuous Modern Dancing' to the Palais Residents' Band, under the direction of Tommy Speakman.

Amateur dramatics was also a popular diversion in 1959. Pride of place must go to the Didsbury Townswomen's Guild Drama Group's production of Women of Twilight that November. The *Manchester Evening News* critic spoke of 'something spicy', with an 'avalanche of bad language'. The actors were praised for 'appearing convincingly immoral'.

And there was, as always, the outing to Maine Road or Old Trafford to watch the Citizens or the Red Devils. The glory days when the two teams would be the best in England were less than a decade away.

THREE

FLYING HIGH

'THE GREATEST RACE THE WORLD HAS EVER SEEN'

The title of 'the world's greatest race' was bestowed by an excited *Daily Express* the day after the race finished in a field near to Burnage station, just over 100 years ago.

Four years earlier, in 1906, the *Daily Mail* had offered a £10,000 prize for the first person to fly from London to Manchester. The time limit was twenty-four hours, the plane had to take off and land within five miles of the Mail offices, and there had to be no more than two stops on the way. At the time it had seemed like a safe enough bet, as, back in 1906, aeroplanes were still struggling to stay aloft for more than a few minutes at a time.

But technology had progressed since then, and there emerged two daring young men, who, between them, pushed back the boundaries of mechanised flight: the Frenchman Louis Paulhan, and the former bicycle mechanic from Hampshire, Claude Grahame-White. They were to compete in the London-Manchester race in a thrilling head-to-head battle.

Paulhan had already made a name for himself in the USA that year. Apart from becoming embroiled in a legal battle over patents with the Wright Brothers, he set a new altitude record of well over 4,000ft, and gave William Randolph Hearst his first trip in an aeroplane.

Grahame-White, aged 30, four years older than Paulhan, had become obsessed with flying since visiting an air show in Reims the previous year. He remained in France (where most of the European aeronautical action of the time could

Winner of the race and £10,000
prize: Frenchman Louis Paulhan.

be found) and, after working in the Blériot factory in Paris, became one of the first Englishmen to gain a pilot's licence.

Preparations for the great race were finalised by mid-April 1910. Both men would be piloting Farman Biplanes. The Farman, the most popular aircraft of the time, was constructed from wood and wire to a boxkite design. Imagine travelling high above the ground in a 40ft-long, lightweight rabbit hutch with wings, a tail and a propeller but no walls, and you get the picture.

As both aviators waited impatiently for the high winds to subside, it was Grahame-White who was the first to bite the bullet, setting off from Wormwood Scrubs at 5.15 a.m. on St George's Day: Saturday 23

April. Paulhan had planned to make the attempt later that week. It was beginning to look like a easy win for the Englishman, but the near gale force winds forced his plane down at Lichfield, Staffordshire, around 50 miles short of his target. Repairs were necessary, and the twenty-four hour limit ticked away. Grahame-White resolved to try again the following Wednesday, 27 April, the same day as Paulhan.

The Frenchman was first away, leaving Hendon at 5.30 in the afternoon. Grahame-White was in the air fifty minutes later. There was some catching up to do, but the Englishman had a highly risky secret weapon: he intended to be the first person ever to fly competitively during the hours of darkness, and thus make up the time on his rival.

At sundown, Grahame-White landed at Roade, Northamptonshire. Paulhan had made it to Lichfield, nearly sixty miles to the north-west, where he spent the night in the same hotel room his rival had the previous Saturday. It looked odds-on a French win, but the Englishman had yet to play his wildcard: at 2.50 a.m. the following morning, Grahame-White took off from Roade. There were lamps and motorcar headlights illuminating the hedgerows, but once these were left behind, the flight was in near pitch darkness. The furnace of a north-bound train below guided him as far as Rugby. He was closing in, and Paulhan had not yet left his hotel.

The lanes and fields around Lichfield were clogged with well-wishers, so that it was just as a grey dawn was breaking, around 4 a.m., when Paulhan reached the take-off field. There was immense excitement in the crowd when someone spotted a light low in the south-eastern sky. Was this Grahame-White, challenging for the lead? Actually no, it turned out to be the planet Venus emerging from behind a cloud!

Paulhan set off, aiming for Crewe, so he could use the tail-wind for the final stretch into Manchester. Behind, and unknown to him, Grahame-White's brave attempt to catch up came to an end at the Warwickshire village of Polesworth. Strong winds and engine trouble had forced him to abandon the race.

So it was that in a grey, drizzly and chilly Manchester dawn, or more precisely in a clover field of Pytha Fold Farm near to Burnage station, a huge crowd saw the arrival of Paulhan's plane. His affected Gallic nonchalance as he waved a 'Voilà!' to the cheering masses betrayed no hint of the cold, exhaustion and relief he later admitted to feeling. When a policeman ran towards the aircraft as it came to a standstill, the pilot thought that he was about to be arrested for trespass, but the bobby's intention was simply to lend Paulhan his overcoat, which the Frenchman gladly accepted.

When asked how he would spend the £10,000 prize money, Paulhan replied that he would invest most of it in the furtherance of air flight.

Both competitors, in fact, having seen the enormous commercial potential of mechanised flight, were scarcely out of the headlines for

Louis Paulhan landing his plane in a field near to Burnage station, 28 April 1910.

DIDSBURY AIRPORT – GATEWAY TO EUROPE

Gallant runner-up, Claude Grahame-White.

the next year or so. Paulhan was to pilot the world's first seaplane. Of the two, Grahame-White drew the larger share of attention. During his American tour later that year, he thought it would be a good idea to land his plane on a busy street in Washington DC. This so impressed the Land of Opportunity that he was fêted rather than arrested.

Back in England he founded the Hendon aerodrome, and made significant contributions to the British Air Force in the First World War. In the same war, Paulhan was decorated for his airborne exploits on the Serbian front.

The blue heritage plaque on a house in Paulhan Road, Burnage, commemorates the London-Manchester flight. In 2010, to mark the centenary of the flight, Manchester Airport named one of its approach roads after the Frenchman.

On Hough End playing fields, where the Greater Manchester Police now train their dogs and horses, there was once an airport. In its heyday, this short-lived (1917-24) air terminal supplied regular flights to London, Blackpool and Dublin, and was by far the most important passenger airport in the area. Ringway wasn't even a twinkle in a planner's eye.

For the last few months of the First World War, Didsbury aerodrome was used for the assembly and test flying of warplanes. Parts were delivered to the nearby station at Alexandra Park, which gave the airfield its alternative name.

After the war, restrictions on civilian aviation were lifted at midnight on 30 April 1919. A lady by the name of Madam Venn, 'costumier and dealer in lady's garments', tried to jump the gun by flying up from London a few hours before the ban ended. Her intention was to deliver, in a blaze of publicity, a display of samples to a fashion trade fair in a

Manchester's first civilian aerodrome on what is now Hough End Fields. Mauldeth Road West crosses the top of the picture.

Manchester hotel. The *Manchester Evening News*, with a dash of pre-feminist chivalry, commented: 'The weather was unfavourable for aerial flights, and any civilian, said the cynics – let alone a lady – would find a flying experience anything but pleasant.'

The perfect end to the story would have been Madam Venn becoming the first non-military pilot to land at the Didsbury aerodrome later that day. Unfortunately, strong headwinds forced her to land at Rugby, from where she travelled the rest of the distance by train. The next day, a heavier aircraft carrying ten passengers and a batch of newspapers landed, having left London some three-and-a-half hours earlier.

By the end of May 1919, Didsbury/Alexandra Park was booming. Regular flights were run to Blackpool, although the cost must have put the trip outside most people's price range: 5 guineas single, and 9 guineas return. A return rail ticket for the same journey cost 7*s* 3*d*.

The success story continued. 1922 was the airport's golden year. On 29 April, to help publicise the imminent Manchester-London passenger flights, an Air Show was held. The afternoon began with a race around the city between three planes, each one sponsored by a local newspaper. Later on, the three teams competed with each other to see how quickly they could burst three airborne balloons by firing air rifles from their plane. Flights were then available to members of the public at £1 a go.

The daily passenger service to Croydon in south London began in June. From Croydon there was a connection to Schiphol Airport in Amsterdam, whence Europe – if not as yet the world – was your oyster.

One of the stipulations of landowner Lord Egerton's lease was that all flying activities would cease five years after the end of the war. By 1924, with Manchester creeping ever southwards and a need for a bigger airport becoming increasingly evident, the Didsbury facility had been closed and demolished. A smart new plaque in the grounds of the Air Cadets centre on Houghend Crescent keeps the memory alive today.

NORTHENDEN AIR PAGEANT

The temporary aerodrome on what is now the Rackhouse housing estate.

Manchester's first commercial, non-military aerodrome was situated on Hough End Fields, just after the First World War. Before Ringway opened in 1938, the city's major airport was over at Chat Moss.

While Chat Moss was being built, however, there was another, temporary, aerodrome on what is now the Rackhouse estate, just to the north of Wythenshawe Park. In the triangle now formed by Sale Road, Wythenshawe Road and Orton Road – an expanse clearly shown on the photograph – a hangar and a few huts transformed the open fields into an airfield. Part of Wythenshawe Park may be seen to the bottom right of the photo. The M/C logo is in the centre of the landing strip. At the time still in Cheshire, the area was designated as being 'in the parish of Northenden, in the County of Chester'.

A de Havilland Cirrus Moth, used for charter flights from Rackhouse.

It was often used for charter flights, open to the public at a shilling a mile. The de Havilland two-seater DH Cirrus Moth would have been used for this service.

The high point (so to speak) of the aerodrome's existence was no doubt the air pageant of April 1929. The early foul weather cleared up in the afternoon, so the several thousand spectators were treated to various displays of derring-do and tomfoolery.

The organisers, Northern Air Lines Limited, had stretched the budget. Refreshments included 10,000 bottles of beer, 3,000 sandwiches, and 1,500 meat pies. Among the aeronautic stars invited were Flt-Lt Webster, holder of the World Speed Record of 312mph, H.A. Brown the professional test pilot and Flash Harry of the aerobatics world, and darling of the skyways Miss Winifred Brown, who also played hockey for England.

Proceedings began with several light aircraft flying in formation from Woodford. Flt-Lt Webster wowed the assembly by flying upside down. Miss Brown made an early statement for equal opportunities by going through her aerobatics repertoire, to the loud delight of the spectators.

However, it was H.A. Brown who stole the show. He performed everything short of a camel spin on his front propellers: 'His machine side-slipped, climbed spirally and then did the falling leaf stunt to the sound of roars of applause,' enthused the *Manchester Evening News* reporter. The incorrigible showman looped the loop a few times as an encore, occasionally drawing cries of concern from those spectators who – needlessly – feared for his safety.

Once the clouds had dispersed, a mock aerial battle was staged, and a sham plane fell in flames from the sky. More comedy was to be had with the sudden entrance onto the airfield of a car, driven by a young couple and garishly decorated with balloons, streamers and 'Just Married' placards. The role of the jilted lover was played by a pilot who swooped from the sky strafing the vehicle with flour bombs. The newlyweds made a run for it, leaving the smoking wreck of the car behind.

The last recorded flight left Rackhouse/Northenden in June 1930, and within eighteen months the area, now belonging to Manchester rather than Cheshire, saw the beginnings of the modern-day overspill estate.

THE YANKEE PAPA MYSTERY

Yankee Papa on Melland
playing fields, Gorton.

Fifty years ago, in April 1961, the world seemed captivated by the idea of manned flight. Yuri Gagarin was being fêted after his inaugural trip into space. BOAC were celebrating their new express freight delivery service to the USA. Ringway Airport had seen another 30 per cent monthly rise in the number of passengers.

So it was a cruel irony that the *Manchester Evening News* also recorded, on 15 April, a fatal air crash on Chorlton Grammar School playing fields (where the Siemens grounds are now, at the corner of Princess Road and Barlow Moor Road).

The cause of the crash was given by the coroner as accidental 'fuel starvation', yet remains a bit of a mystery, especially as the main fuel tank was later discovered to be full. The pilot, Roland Longhurst, from Hampshire, was just 22 years old, but was experienced enough to own a commercial pilot's licence. The plane had had a new engine fitted a year earlier, and had been serviced at Barton airport on the morning of the tragedy. A few minutes before the crash, Longhurst had radioed the Ringway control tower to report all was well.

The plane was a single-engined Auster, which had seen good service in its eight-year life. Its registration was G-AGYP, so was affectionately known as 'Yankee Papa' by the plane spotters at Ringway, for whom it was a familiar sight for much of the 1950s.

Yankee Papa, owned for a while by the former 'Airviews' company (no connection with the present business), had been used for advertising: you may have seen the black and yellow *Manchester Evening News* banner fluttering behind it. Other uses included aerial photography, flying lessons, both in Manchester and Portsmouth, and chartered pleasure flights. An avid plane spotter recalled it as the first plane he ever logged at Ringway airport in July 1956.

The photograph, however, presents another mystery. Here is Yankee Papa in happier days, having made a successful landing on Melland playing fields, Gorton. The Civil Aviation Authorities' archives don't cover any year before 1972, and my enquiries about the incident have proven fruitless. What job was the plane performing at the time? Why did the pilot land? Who was he? Who took the photo? Was there any problem in taking off again? It may be relevant that Yankee Papa was owned from April 1953 to March 1955 by a Thomas Mason, who lived in Marshall Road, Levenshulme, less than a mile from Melland fields.

So, over to you, readers. Were you there when the plane landed on the football pitches? Or do you know of someone who was?

FROM CHAPEL-OF-EASE TO EASYJET

For 400 years the most exciting event to have taken place in the hamlet of Ringway was the turfing-out of non-conformists from the Anglican Chapel in 1721. There was a bit of a scuffle, and the Dissenters held their services in a nearby barn before moving on to Hale.

Consecrated in 1515 as a chapel-of-ease, Ringey Chapel was intended as a convenient place of worship for those who lived in the depths of farmland Cheshire, and who were unable to make the trek to the church at Bowden. The present building was consecrated as St Mary's Church in 1895. Ringway clung to its rural quiescence and isolation for over four centuries ... and then the airport arrived.

Manchester's major civilian aerodrome had occupied three previous sites: Hough End Fields, Rackhouse (Northenden), and Barton. As the metropolis sprawled and the population grew, it became clear by the 1930s that not even the sizeable Barton could cater for the burgeoning demand for air travel.

The clincher was a visit from the Director of the Dutch airline KLM. He declared himself unimpressed with the space and facilities at Barton, and stated that his choice for north-west England's KLM base would be Liverpool. Predictably, this stung Manchester City Council into looking for a site for a new airport.

The area north of the Bollin, on Ringway Chapel's doorstep, was preferred to four alternatives: Bury, Mobberley, Audenshaw, and an extension to Barton. The reasons were: the firmer clay soil; the building of Princess Parkway, which would allow easier access from central Manchester; the distance from an industrial centre, so less likelihood of fog; and the availability of a large expanse of the Cheshire plain devoid of humps and bumps and man-made obstructions.

Cheshire County Council took the decision to the High Court, but government backing for the scheme won the day, and construction started in November 1935.

Ringway Chapel, looking much the same as it did over
a hundred years ago. (Graham Phythian)

During the digging for the foundations, some large bones were unearthed. Rumours of dinosaur remains drew palaeontologists to the site like a magnet, but interest waned when it was discovered that the bones had belonged to an elephant. The animal had been a member of a travelling circus, and on its death had been buried there by its owners.

Ringway Airport was officially opened in June 1938. Initially mainly employed for domestic flights (plus the reactivated KLM link with Amsterdam), the passenger turnover in the first year was a mere 4,000. Nowadays it's around 18 million.

The phenomenal growth from minor aerodrome to International Airport can be followed by looking at samples from the timeline:

Concorde (1976-2000), now gracefully retired in a hangar at Manchester Airport. (Jon West)

1947: British European Airways starts to operate
1953: First regular transatlantic service: Manchester–New York (Sabena from Brussels)
1954: Name officially changed to Manchester Airport: 1 million post-war passengers
1962: HRH Prince Philip opens new terminal
1969: Main runway extended; first transatlantic jet service to New York
1970: Ringway Chapel closes;
used as a storeroom and studio until 2011
1976: Concorde lands at Manchester
1981: Laker Skytrain service to Miami
1987: Boeing 747 service to Orlando and Barbados: 'international gateway'
1989: Terminal 1A (later Terminal 3) opened by Diana, Princess of Wales
1993: Opening of Terminal 2 and the railway link
2004: Twenty million passengers: transport interchange facility opened

Recommended is the guided tour of Concorde, housed in a converted hangar in the Aviation Viewing Park at the end of Wilmslow Old Road. The supersonic airliner may have been an economic hot potato, but it's still a beautiful and imposing piece of technology.

And a few hundred yards down the lane, while the modern world whizzes and roars around it, the recently re-consecrated Ringway Chapel stands serenely among its trees and gravestones, looking much as it did a century or more ago.

FOUR

MURDERS AND OTHER MISDEMEANOURS

WHO KILLED MARY MOORE?

Between Chorlton's Horse and Jockey and Bowling Green pubs, just beyond the open space, there is a lych gate, remnant of the demolished chapel. The chapel's old gravestones now serve as flagstones, and just inside the gate one inscription reads:

Mary Wife of Joseph Moore who was robbed and cruelly murdered at Withington on the 19th of June 1838 in the 49th Year of her Age.

These stark and poignant details have been researched by local historian Andy Simpson, and thanks to his labours, we can reconstruct the events of that dark day. The full story is given in Andy's excellent book on mid-nineteenth century Chorlton.

Mary Moore was employed at Dog House Farm, which was roughly where Caistor Close is now, off Alexandra Road South. She lived by Chorlton Green, and on market days would walk the couple of miles to the farm, where employee Thomas Hooley would be waiting for her in the cart. Their destination was Smithfield Market in the centre of Manchester, where Mary's job was to sell the fruit from the Dog House Farm orchards. Since it was her responsibility to bring the proceeds from the sales back to the farm, hers was a position of trust.

Manchester was the boom town of the decade, and bustling Smithfield Market, on the corner of Shude Hill and Swan Street, and surrounded by the racket of cotton mills and engineering works, would have done a roaring trade that day, selling produce from the city's many outlying farms. Mary was to confide in a friend that she had had 'a good market', which suggests that she had sold all the produce, making an estimated £3, a considerable sum for those days.

Although Mary had arranged with Thomas that they would meet at Brook Street for the journey home, for reasons unknown she failed to turn up, so Thomas returned to Dog House Farm alone. Mary walked back, and was last seen round about 2 p.m., on the lane a few hundred yards from the farm. She was never to arrive.

Her body was found the next day; face-down in a water-filled ditch a couple of hundred yards from her destination. She had been bludgeoned to death by two blows from a blunt instrument on the back of her head. The money from the market, her basket and umbrella were all missing.

The three-week-long inquest was held at Withington's Red Lion pub. Early suspicion, whetted by sensationalist newspaper reports, fell on four men who had been seen playing pitch-and-toss by the entrance to the field in which Mary had been found. The case against them collapsed, however, when it was proven that they had left the scene well before noon.

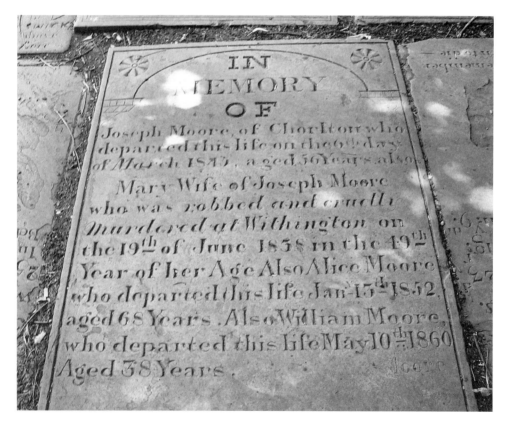

Mary Moore's gravestone at Chorlton Green. (Graham Phythian)

The Red Lion pub in Withington, where the inquest took place. (*Manchester Evening News* publications)

Attention now shifted to ex-marine William Hodge, a former worker at Dog House Farm. According to one witness, Hodge had been asking questions about Mary Moore's usual route back from market, and whether the sale of orchard fruit from the farm made much money. Although this was hotly denied by Hodge, there was further damning evidence: on the day of the murder the ex-marine had been seen hiding something in a hedge on Jackson's Lane in Hulme. The cache turned out to be two parcels containing a total of £3.

Hodge was pronounced guilty, and taken to the Lancashire County Jail at Kirkdale, to await trial at Liverpool assizes.

A CHORLTON MURDER MYSTERY

In 1876, before the coming of the railways to South Manchester, Chorlton was mostly farmland parcelled off by lanes and hedgerows. A popular pub with the farm workers was the Royal Oak on Barlow Moor Road (on the site of today's pub, which was built around it before it was demolished). Among the pub's clientele were the Habron brothers, John, Frank and William, who supplemented their legal earnings with the occasional spot of poaching on the nearby estates. They were also known to the police for their drunk and disorderly antics. The local bobby, PC Nicholas Cock, a young bachelor and an especially keen and vigilant officer of the law, had had run-ins with the Habron brothers, leading to their arrest and conviction for several petty crimes.

One evening in the Royal Oak, in the summer of 1876, the youngest of the brothers, 18-year-old William, was overheard maligning PC Cock – uttering threats of somehow getting even with him, or even putting an end to him. Because of what transpired later that year, this bit of bravado turned out to be a big mistake.

It was 1 August, around midnight, and PC Cock was walking his beat. He was approaching the corner of Seymour Grove and Upper Chorlton Road – outside where the Seymour pub was later to stand, and where the new flats are today. His remit was to reach the corner at midnight, then retrace his steps back into Chorlton. With him was a friend, John Simpson, the son of a well-to-do lawyer who lived on Upper Chorlton Road, across the border in Whalley Range. They stopped on the corner to finish their conversation. While they were talking, a man walked past them on his way towards Chorlton. The policeman and the lawyer's son then bid each other goodnight, and went their separate ways. Simpson was about a hundred yards away when he heard two gunshots and a cry of 'Murder!' He ran back to the corner, where he saw Cock slumped by the wall, bleeding profusely from a chest wound. There was no sign of his assailant. The shots had also attracted two Whalley Range policemen to the scene. Cock was placed on a passing dust-cart, and he was taken to a nearby doctor's house, where he died half an hour later.

The dying policeman was able to say that his attacker had 'lain in wait for him'. It was a detail that would be made much of by the prosecution. Knowing of the bad blood between Cock and the Habrons, the police were round at their outhouse dwelling within the hour.

Some gun cartridges, similar to the one that had killed PC Cock, were found in William Habron's possession. An examination of William's boots seemed to show that they matched one of the footprints left near to the crime. The young farm worker was arrested and charged with murder. The trial was set for the end of November 1876.

At first, the prosecution seemed to hold all the aces: the apparent evidence of the boot prints and cartridges, along with Habron's public threats against PC Cock, seemed conclusive.

As the two-day trial progressed, however, the case against William started to crumble. The cartridges were found to be similar, but not identical. The police declared themselves to be less than 100 per cent sure about the footprint evidence.

And it was strange that Cock had not identified his assailant before he died, even though William was surely well known to him. Most crucially of all, who was the man that had been seen walking towards the crime scene a few minutes before the murder? One witness described him as 'young, about 22', but John Simpson, Cock's friend, described him as 'elderly'.

The doubts weren't enough to persuade the jury, who, after a short deliberation, found William Habron guilty of murder. Because of his youth, however, they recommended life imprisonment. The judge, leaving clemency to the Home Office, pronounced the death sentence. Habron continued to protest his innocence.

The trial had excited nationwide interest, and, unnoticed in the packed public gallery, one Charles Peace, seasoned burglar and general rogue, had been following proceedings more avidly than most. On hearing the verdict and sentence, Peace left the courtroom and returned to his native Sheffield, where the next day, in his cups, he entertained a pub audience by playing tunes on a poker. He had good reason to celebrate, as it was he who had murdered PC Cock.

Drawn to Chorlton by tales of rich pickings, he was the 'elderly man' seen by John Simpson. He had walked past the policeman and his friend whilst they were chatting, then hidden in the garden of the first house past the corner, waiting for the coast to clear. Cock, noticing the open gate, had entered the garden to investigate. Confronted, Peace fired a warning shot while Cock, true to character, came at him with his truncheon. Peace shot the policeman in the chest, before making his escape down one of the myriad of farm tracks.

The story's ending is mostly a happy one. Two days before his appointment with the hangman, Habron's sentence was commuted to life imprisonment. Then, three years later, Charles Peace was arrested for another murder, for which he was condemned to death. Realising there was no escape this time, Peace admitted to the murder of PC Cock,

Charles Peace, rogue, burglar
... and murderer.

even drawing a convincing map of the shooting, so there could be no doubt to his guilt.

William Habron was granted a free pardon, and awarded £800 (over £160,000 nowadays) in compensation.

A POLICEMAN'S LOT

Every community has its lunatic fringe, and the townships of South Manchester in mid-Victorian times were no exception. The bobbies on the beat, however, were, for the most part, commendably vigilant in bringing the wrongdoers to book. Were they overzealous? Would a stern telling-off have done the trick just as well? Judge for yourselves.

John Coulson owned a fish and poultry shop on Moss Lane West in the 1880s. The shop was on the north side of the street, in the area newly absorbed into Manchester, while the southern side of the street was still in Lancashire. One evening Mr Coulson, much the worse for drink, was parading up and down in front of his shop in what was deemed by a passing policeman to be a disorderly manner. The shop owner, quite reasonably, was told to get off home. Now, since the policeman belonged to the Lancashire constabulary, Coulson referred to his version of the US State Line law, asserting, 'County bobbies

have no right on this side of the road.' Big mistake. The magistrate at the County Police Court, stating that it was a 'perfectly ridiculous idea', fined Coulson 20 shillings.

The police were especially keen on arresting footpath-blockers. In 1886, a tricyclist using the pedestrian way alongside the road in Withington was fined 2/6*d*. Two runners jogging along a path ('not racing, just practising') between Ladybarn and Burnage were fined 5 shillings. Two young lads playing leapfrog on a footpath in Didsbury were deemed to be obstructing the way, and were fined 2/6*d*.

The tricyclist may have had an excuse, since, around the same time, two horse and cart drivers were arrested for racing along Palatine Road. The policeman estimated their speed at 'between 14 and 15 miles per hour.' The accused gave their speed at around 8-9mph, and said they were 'only larking'. The magistrate was unmoved, and fined them 10 shillings, plus costs.

Illicit gambling, especially amongst the young, was also a common target for the bobby on the beat. In May 1887, three children were engaged in the illegal activity of pitch and toss outside the cricket ground at Old Trafford. They switched to marbles as soon as the policeman strode into view, little realising that the officer of the law had been spying on them from behind a nearby wall. The lads appeared in Strangeways Police Court, where they were fined 5 shillings each.

A cart is escorted to Newton Street police station, *c.* 1880. (Greater Manchester Police)

Despite the police presence, some petty crimes of that time were never solved. Forty-eight bottles of lemonade were stolen from a Didsbury tennis club. During a concert and 'living waxworks' at St Agnes' Church, Levenshulme, a bunch of local youngsters created their own amusement by setting fire to some old furniture in the vestry. A number of fake florins were found in circulation in Didsbury in 1889. A pair of trousers was stolen from a farmhouse in Back Levenshulme. In each case, the perpetrators were never discovered.

At least the public could rest easy in the knowledge that they were being protected from underage gamblers, footpath tricyclists, and leapfrogging youths.

CRIMES AND PECCADILLOES

There is a tendency to idealise the rural scene, just as there is a tendency to idealise the past. Throughout most of the nineteenth century, South Manchester was mostly open countryside, dotted with villages and farmsteads that were later to grow and coalesce into the suburbs. An idyllic setting? Perhaps; but there was more to the idyll than met the eye.

To the north of Fog Lane in Didsbury, where the park is today, was pastureland belonging to farmer Josiah Bethell. He owned a herd of cows, many of whom, one day in 1885, took a fancy to the neighbouring market gardener's crop (about where Old Broadway is now). Hunger proving stronger than the intervening fences, the cattle invaded the crop fields and, it was alleged in court, polished off forty-eight dozen cabbages and cauliflowers. Bethell was ordered to pay £2 in damages and costs, and instructed to exercise more efficient cow crowd control.

In those days, semi-rural South Manchester had its share of crimes and misdemeanours. A few shopkeepers had found ways to make an illicit shilling or two. Watered-down milk from a Heaton Chapel farm was discovered in circulation, and the perpetrator was fined a hefty £5. Four shops in Ardwick, apparently in cahoots, were convicted of selling 'butterine', or butter adulterated with 'foreign fat'.

The main cause of public nuisance in the area at the time seems to have been the demon drink. Besides the many drunk and cursing/begging/disorderly cases, a couple of instances at least show an attempt at some ingenuity. A woman working as a cook in a well-to-do house in Didsbury was discovered by her employer helping herself to beer in the cellar. To access the liquor more quickly, she had turned the barrel on its side, and had positioned herself on the floor with her mouth under the tap. The witty headline in the *South Manchester Gazette* for 14 November 1885 read: 'DIDN'T RUN FAST ENOUGH'.

William Clegg of Longsight was rather the worse for drink when he entered the local police station to complain of someone breaking into his house. It may have seemed like a good idea at the time, but the police lost interest when it transpired that the alleged housebreakers were Clegg's landlords demanding overdue rent!

The new phenomenon of houses with front gardens attracted the wrong sort of attention in Levenshulme. Early Sunday morning was the time for flower thieves to swoop. The delightfully non-PC report in the local newspaper spoke of the 'well-kept gardens wilfully poached upon by unwashed blackguards.'

The cheekiest attempt at a scam was carried out in January 1886 by the elderly Ellen Murgatroyd, living in Rusholme at the time, who persuaded two young serving girls that she could foretell the future and 'rule the planets'. They crossed her palm with silver – eight shillings, to be exact – and the self-styled prophetess said she would be back with a full horoscope within the hour. Surprise, surprise, she didn't show up, so the serving girls went to the police, and the prototype Mystic Meg was arrested later that day.

MRS WORRALL AND THE CURATE

Scandal has always got the public salivating. When it involves the wife of a wealthy local businessman and a member of the cloth, the knives and forks come out with the relish.

In the 1880s, Henry Worrall, having made a fortune from his Salford Dye Works, settled with his young and attractive wife at the opulent Crimsworth House on Upper Chorlton Road, in leafy Whalley Range. The marriage produced three sons in the first three years, which was ideal for carrying on the business dynasty. The 1891 census shows the members of the family as Henry (39), wife Louisa (34), Philip (10), Stephen (9), Bertram (8), and daughter Louisa Grace (4). The household had a nurse, waitress, cook, two housemaids and a kitchen maid.

The surface affluence, however, hid an increasingly dysfunctional marriage. An undemonstrative husband who immersed himself in work, and a wife trying to deal with the loss of her first flush of youth: with hindsight we can see a Madame Bovary tale brewing, a recipe for disaster.

Moreover, Henry had a violent and insecure streak, and it later came to light that he had struck his wife on at least three occasions. Or there was the Cold War, in which the husband wrote notes to the wife whilst they were both living under the same roof, as they weren't talking! Eventually, to quote Mr Worrall, they 'ceased to live as husband and wife'.

Enter the Reverend Hugh William Jones, curate of the Worralls' church of St Mary's, Hulme. Jones was an athletic young man, fond of golf and cricket, and it wasn't long before Louisa Worrall was making eyes at him.

Matters reached a head in the summer of 1893. At first it was innocent enough: Jones accompanied Mrs Worrall to the church-sponsored *tableaux vivants* at Fallowfield, in which famous works of art were recreated by tastefully arranged groups of people. Mrs Worrall took part in one of them, but, despite the dubious reputation of the art form in some circles, so far everything seems to have been above board.

Then Louisa and the curate started to spend a good deal of time together, especially when Mr Worrall was away on business. The husband's suspicions were aroused by an ardent look bestowed by his wife on the Reverend during a dinner party at Crimsworth. The next day there was a near-farcical episode in which Worrall tried to rip a letter out of his wife's hands, correctly surmising that it was for Jones. Mrs Worrall tried to tear it up and swallow it, but, after a violent scene, her husband was able to retrieve enough of it to read the following: 'Darling … you are the dearest … I could squeeze you all to pieces … ' The letter was signed 'Fuzzy-Buzzy', which, in the circumstances, was a bit of a giveaway.

Worrall immediately forbade Jones from visiting Crimsworth, and there began a chapter of secret assignations between Mrs Worrall and the curate. Jones would appear on the road outside the house and signal the all-clear with a flap of his handkerchief. Golf lessons on the nearby Manley Park links segued into hitherto unexplored use of the grassy slopes around the bunkers. When the family were holidaying at Saltburn near Whitby in August, Jones turned up (minus the dog-collar) to find that Mrs Worrall had arranged an extra room for a night. Her husband had left on business, and a maid was delegated to look after the children, whilst the couple, to borrow the choice wording from

Crimsworth House, home to Henry Worrall's family and domestic servants. The building was demolished in 1987, after having served as Preparatory Department for Whalley Range High School. The Manley Park golf course was a short distance down College Road. (Philip Lloyd)

the *Observer*, indulged their 'passion that was not of an innocent nature'.

The inevitable divorce case, greedily documented by the newspapers, followed, and the decree became absolute in January 1896. The court order gave custody of the daughter –Louisa Grace – to Mr Worrall, with no access granted to her mother. Mrs Worrall, now living in Brighton, at first refused to comply, but, when threatened with confiscation of her property, she was forced to make the painful decision to let her daughter go.

Henry Worrall, even wealthier after a business merger in 1899, married Miss Greener, Headmistress of Whalley Range High School for Girls. Crimsworth became the school's Preparatory Department before being demolished in 1987. Now the only remains of the great house are the stone pillars on Upper Chorlton Road, marking the entrance to the driveway.

Crimsworth House also served as a nursery. The following reminiscences were contributed by Janet Phillips:

I think it was 1957 when I started there as a three-year-old. The entrance was on the corner of College Road and Upper Chorlton Road. As you made your way up the path towards the house, there was a large brick sand pit on the left-hand side. The building was surrounded by grass and gardens.

Outside, to the right of the entrance, were a climbing frame and a set of monkey bars. I remember playing 'I'm the king of the castle and you're the dirty rascal' on the climbing frame, and being able to do a somersault on the monkey bars.

My first classroom was in the basement, there being a 'Wendy house' to the right of the room as you came through the door: that's all I can visualise of that room. I do remember getting some hard kind of biscuit (maybe an Ovaltine rusk) each day. I know I used to like them.

In the afternoons, if it was a nice day, we had a sleep outside on the hill, under some trees. We each had a little metal fold up bed, with one of those school grey wool blankets – ugggh, scratchy or what. Sometimes you wouldn't feel like sleeping. I can remember my friend and I secretly whispering and giggling with each other.

Of course, playing out was heaven as I only had a backyard at home. We had the run of the grounds at the back of the house. The ground sloped down away from the house, with two paths running parallel either side of a lawn, and rhododendron bushes or something similar at the side of those. At the bottom end were more bushes and woody type land. I used to love playing in the bushes. I seem to remember playing in what must have been the old stables, if the weather wasn't too good. I also have vague recollections of going in a small room upstairs (maybe the first floor) for a story. There was some kind of window seat in there.

My second classroom was on the ground floor to the right as you went in, where I was taught to write my name.

After I left there I went to Manley Park School, which was an old wooden building, later moving to the newer junior building which was built at the bottom end of the grounds of Crimsworth, back where I'd started.

I just wish I'd gone back there to take some photographs and look round before the place was demolished.

RED SHIFT

Imagine it happening today. A top-ranking Premiership football club is found guilty by the Football Association of making illegal payments to players (I know, as if) and, as punishment, the club is cripplingly fined, all of the first team squad is banned from playing for them ever again, and the manager and the chairman are also suspended for life.

Incredible? Yet that's what happened to Manchester City in the purge of 1906.

At the centre of the storm was the gifted Welsh international winger Billy Meredith. In the days when the maximum footballer's wage was legally set at £4 a week, Meredith had been more outspoken than most in criticising the system.

Clubs, of course, had found ways round the wages straitjacket, and illegal bonuses (with, in some cases, a subsequent doctoring of the books) were the rule rather than the exception amongst the country's most successful sides. The only unwritten code was that the practice remained hidden from the eagle eyes of the Football League and the FA. Or, as Meredith put it, 'Clubs are not punished for breaking the law. They are punished for being found out.'

City in 1904 were easily the leading team in Manchester, winning the FA Cup and challenging for the League Championship until the final weeks of the season. At the time, United were still in the Second Division. City's achievements drew the attention of the FA investigators, who asked to see the club's books. Quite rightly suspecting that City's success was in no small measure due to under-the-table payments, the FA men could find no evidence of this in the records, but there was a definite whiff of creative accountancy having been at work. A couple of forged receipts relating to the signing on of two new players resulted in a £250 fine and the Hyde Road ground being closed for a month.

This was only the beginning of City's woes. In April 1905, with the Manchester side pushing once again for the League title, Meredith was overheard offering a bribe to an Aston Villa player during a top of the table clash. The Welshman was later to insist it was only meant as a joke, but

Manchester City FC, FA Cup winners in 1904. Within two years, the team would be obliterated. Billy Meredith is seated in the middle

Paris a couple of years previously, but notably without a British presence. London had just made a successful bid for the 1908 Olympics, which, of course, were still strictly amateur. At exactly the same time that the FA Commission was deliberating City's punishment, King Edward VII, patron of the Football Association, was a conspicuous figure at the 1906 intercalated Olympic Games in Athens. The sporting establishment seems to have felt the need to show the world that England still represented the amateur ideal, by dramatically being seen to put its house in order. City were handy scapegoats.

the FA failed to see the funny side and suspended Meredith for a season.

In the meantime, the FA were keeping a close watch on City's wages dealings. After a few months of scrupulous investigation and several inquisitions of players and officials, the whole can of worms was spilled. It was discovered that many players had regularly been paid in excess of the statutory £4 maximum. The FA's reaction (some said overreaction) took the sporting world's breath away. At a stroke City lost seventeen top players, the services of two vital managerial staff, and through fines and ground closure, most of their estimated £50,000 cash assets.

The reasons for the unusual harshness of the sentence may probably be traced to the sensitive situation English sport found itself in at the time. FIFA had been founded in

Meredith served his two seasons' suspension and then, along with three other ex-City first team players, found employment across town playing for United. By then in the First Division, United won the League in 1908 and 1911, and were Cup winners in 1909. They moved into their new home at Old Trafford and the rest, as they say, is history.

PENSIONS AND PURSUITS

Just over a hundred years ago, on Friday, 6 January 1911, South Manchester post offices were for the first time the scene of the Old Age Pension queues.

If you were aged 70 or over with no other significant means of income, you were entitled to claim up to five shillings a week. This doesn't sound like much, but with a large loaf costing around 2*d*, and a hundredweight of coal at about a shilling, the pension was, to quote an employer of the time, 'a wise allocation of public funds'. Thank the Liberal Government, whose 1911 cabinet was studded with such stars as Winston Churchill and Lloyd George.

Perhaps it was apt that the date was also Twelfth Night, the festival traditionally associated with social inversion and the Season of Misrule. To be sure, there was no wrinklies' revolution brewing, but a definite shift in the social landscape was in evidence. The old no longer had to depend on their family or live in fear of the workhouse.

An elderly lady in the Levenshulme post office queue was heard to exclaim, 'I've sacked my old man!' Upon being asked what she meant, she explained, 'My husband is younger than I am, and he has continually taunted me with being an old woman. Now I've got a pension I've sacked him, because with my five shillings pension and what I can earn by nursing children, I shall be all right.' Then the gleefully delivered punchline: 'And my husband is too young for a pension!'

If you were younger, fitter, and not burdened with a conscience, there were other less legal methods of adding to your income. In the new suburbia of Withington and Whalley Range, the practice of breaking and entering was enjoying some popularity at the time. This also often involved the innovative sport of garden hedge hurdling, pursued by a vigilante or two.

The same edition of the *Manchester Evening News* which reported on the new pension also carried a story which bore the headline 'Exciting Chases'.

A burglar, described as 'well dressed', was seen leaving a house on Withington Road. He had stolen a pair of boots, which he dropped as soon as the cry of 'Stop thief!' was uttered by the lady of the house. Two passers-by gave chase as far as Moss Lane West, where the fugitive was caught and handed over to the police.

A pair of thieves – one to keep watch, the other to break in and fill the large pockets of his overcoat with loot – targeted a house in Amherst Road, Withington. All was going according to plan until the local bobby, PC Kearton, happened to walk past the front of the house. The thief who was standing guard gave a whistle and ran to the back. This rather gave the game away, and Kearton followed, blowing his whistle. He pursued the burglars across gardens and hedges, accompanied by a couple of 'have a go' local lads.

The posse finally caught up with the thieves near Linden Grove, and the overcoat, pockets stashed with silver spoons and jewellery, was found abandoned in a garden in Amherst Road.

All the failed burglars received three months' imprisonment – not quite the intended outcome of their brief Season of Misrule.

FIVE

HIGHWAYS AND BYWAYS

STOCKPORT ROAD STORIES

Wherever the Romans pushed the boundaries of Empire, they built roads.

Running straight as a die across the landscape, the surfaced highways were indelible evidence of the technology and resources of the new power in the land. They were also a fearsomely efficient means of shifting troops. The natives thought twice, if at all, about kicking up a fuss if they knew that within hours a heavily armed cohort could come hammering up the road.

At least six of these expressways converged on the fort at Manchester (or rather *Mamucium* – 'the land of the breast-shaped hills'). To the south-east, the fort was linked to the spa town of *Aquae Arnemetiae* (Buxton to me and you). We now call the road the A6, and it still more or less follows the ancient route.

Stockport Road, as it passes through Levenshulme, used to be known as the Roman Road, when it wasn't High Street or the London Road. Over the centuries, this short stretch of thoroughfare has been witness to a fascinating collage of events and changes.

Levenshulme around 1500 has been described as 'scattered farmhouses and a few isolated cottages bordering on the old Stockport lane (for road it could not then be called).' Nevertheless, the Roman Road was an important link between the two market towns of Manchester and Stockport. The Midway House pub (now a cash-and-carry) had been licensed premises since Shakespeare's day, offering a watering-hole at the halfway point for those making the usual footslog between the towns. Interestingly, cattle making the same trek didn't

Stockport Road, Levenshulme, 1904. (Manchester Central
Library Local Image Collection: ref.m39484)

Stockport Road today. (Graham Phythian)

get their water trough – situated by Black Brook, on the border with Heaton Chapel – until 1885.

The introduction of a turnpike in 1724 helped defray the cost of repairs and upkeep. The toll bar was situated on the corner of Slade Lane. Some twenty years later this was the route followed, south to Derby and then back again, by Bonnie Prince Charlie and his supporters.

Sympathiser Thomas Sydall lived at nearby Slade Hall, until brought to London for trial. The King's magistrates taking a dim view of Jacobite tendencies, Sydall was duly hanged, chopped into bits and decapitated, his head being displayed at the Royal Exchange in central Manchester.

Meanwhile, back on the Roman Road, things were speeding up. Ten years after the Jacobite incident the new 'Flying Coach' was being advertised: 'However incredible it may appear, this coach will actually (barring accidents) arrive in London 4½ days after leaving Manchester.' The journey would have set you back two guineas. For comparison, the average daily wage for a farm worker at the time was around two shillings.

Levenshulme Wakes saw the usual annual entertainments. One such was a foot race along Stockport Road, from the Railway Inn to St Peter's Church and back again, after which the competitors had to eat a bowl of scalding hot porridge. The first to complete the task – presumably regurgitation disqualified you – won a silver watch.

The Manchester-Birmingham railway was built in 1834, but the road had to wait until the other end of Victoria's reign before it enjoyed the services of an electric tram. The terminus was at the Jolly Carter pub, which once stood on Black Brook Bridge.

The Buxton Turnpike Trust expired in the mid-nineteenth century, and upkeep of the Roman Road was intermittent until Levenshulme became part of Manchester in 1909.

In the twenty-first century, the Stockport Road in M19 is a busy thoroughfare, a vibrant and colourful mix of cultures fully in keeping with Manchester's cosmopolitan reputation.

THE BATTLE FOR LAPWING LANE

'Disgusted of Didsbury' may well be a suburban myth, but he has his origins firmly in South Manchester tradition. Take a look at the following entertaining spat, lifted verbatim from the 'Letters' page of the *Manchester Courier* in October 1896:

Sir – The other day on turning the corner of Palatine-road by the tram terminus, I saw that the old 'Lapwing-lane' had become 'Cavendish-road'. By whose instrumentality the change was known [sic] I know not, but I would like to know for what end the unique and poetical name of 'Lapwing-lane' has been changed to the prosaic and common place name of 'Cavendish-road', a specimen of which already exists in Manchester.

Doubtless some reason could be given by the authors of the outrage. Yours, etc., JOSEPHUS (13/10/1896)

Sir – I was pleased to see that some-one had the courage to find fault with the new name for the familiar old Lapwing-lane, and should like to inquire whose taste it was that procured it. Why should one or two of us have the power to annoy old residents by putting up ridiculous names at the corner of the road for everyone to adopt 'nolens volens'? Yours, etc., AN OLD ACQUAINTANCE (14/10/1896)

The following day, a long letter from a John Baird attempted to put the question of local name changes into a historical context. He pointed out that Lapwing Lane was originally called Lapwing Hall Lane, after the farm that used to be situated where the junction with Palatine Road later stood. He goes on: Fog Lane initially had an extra 'g', since 'fogg' was an old North Country word meaning moss, peat, or coarse pasture, which perfectly described the land across which ran the old path to Burnage. Mr Baird ventured to suggest that the change to Cavendish Road was in anticipation of the extension of the road across the fields to Chorlton.

Of interest here is the fact that if you look at a modern map of South Manchester, take a ruler and lay it along Corkland Road in Chorlton and look south-east, Cavendish Road in Withington is on exactly the same line. Sure enough, Corkland Road used to bear the name Cavendish Road until after the Second World War, by which time the original plan to link them up had long since been dropped, negotiations with the Egerton estate having ended some time before.

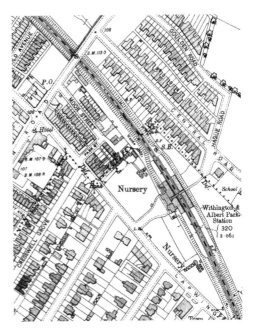

Battleground ... Lapwing Lane (after that brief 1896 re-naming) extends as far as the crossroads with Burton Road, beyond which it becomes Cavendish Road. The hotel at the crossroads is Mr Coombs's inn, The Midland. The walls of the funnel-shaped approach to the old railway station are still standing. The tram terminus mentioned in the first letter was at the junction at the bottom right-hand corner of the map section. (Ordnance Survey 1905)

Meanwhile, back in 1896, the battle of words continued:

Sir – A majority of the Withington District Council, having decided to alter the name of Lapwing-lane to that of Cavendish-road, it is unfair on the part of 'An Old Acquaintance' to make the officials responsible ...
Yours, etc., OBSERVER
(16/10/1896)

Before Withington and Didsbury were absorbed into Manchester in 1904, local decisions were made at the Council Offices on Lapwing Lane ... or was it Cavendish Road?

The old Withington and Didsbury Town Hall on Lapwing Lane, now owned by a media and events company. (Graham Phythian)

Sir – If, as it appears, the village folk object so much to this snobbish innovation, why should they not try to cancel it?
Yours, etc., AN OLD INHABITANT
(20/10/1896)

'Snobbish innovation' hit the nail on the head. It later came to light that Mr Coombs, the Council chairman and landlord of the Midland Hotel on Lapwing Lane, fancied a more aristocratic-sounding address for his hostelry. The decision in favour of the change to Cavendish Road was a close one, with evidence of factions and tactical voting.

The public indignation was noted, however, and six months later the issue was put to the vote once more. This time it went 17 to 1 in favour of restoring the old name, with only Mr Coombs stubbornly hanging on to his aspiration.

The old Withington and Didsbury Town Hall is still standing, now a Grade II listed building owned by an events and media company. It is situated definitely – and definitively – on Lapwing Lane.

FROM FARM TRACK TO FLYOVER

The A5103 (Princess Road/Parkway) sweeps south from Whalley Range

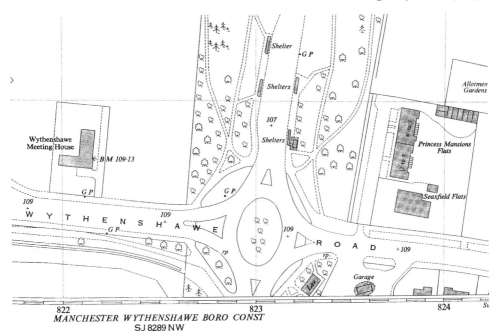

Part of an OS map from 1956 showing the junction of Princess Parkway and Wythenshawe Road, where the motorway flyover is today. The Quaker Meeting House to the west of the junction is still there, and remains untouched by time. (Ordnance Survey)

and Withington, crossing the Mersey before merging seamlessly into the M60/M56 network. By the time it crosses high above Wythenshawe Road by the Airport Britannia Hotel, this roaring thoroughfare has already reached motorway status.

You might be forgiven for thinking that this was always the main route southward from central Manchester. Not so.

In the beginning there was the path, linking Kenworthy Farm to Baguley Hall. Then in the 1930s there was the need to serve the new Wythenshawe estate, so Princess Road was extended south from Barlow Moor Road. The country lane that passed by Christ Church,

Henlys petrol station and garage, at the corner of Princess Parkway and Wythenshawe Road, *c.* 1960. It was demolished when the subway was built. (Northenden Civic Society)

51

Didsbury, was widened and upgraded to form Princess Parkway, which joined Altrincham Road south-east of Wythenshawe Park. And originally, it was intended to take it no further: a wide, tree-lined access avenue, a parkland gateway to the estate.

Then came the airport, which grew and grew, demanding an arterial route south from Manchester. With the flood of traffic came problems, chief of which was how pedestrians were to cross the increasingly busy highway.

I can recall the roundabout with its well-kept greenery, and the little Henlys petrol station. Opposite, where the Britannia is now, were the red brick garden-ensconced Princess Mansion Flats, or as we used to call them, 'the posh flats', to distinguish them from the grim and stuccoed behemoths on the overspill estate.

Everything was on the one level in those days, and traversing the junction on foot (if you didn't fancy dodging between the cars and buses) was by a zebra crossing just to the north of the roundabout. Traffic got heavier, so the crossing was replaced by a footbridge: a partial solution, as the

A bus comes a cropper in the subway. The Britannia Hotel is in the background. (Northenden Civic Society: photo by Denis Thorpe)

steps were a barrier to pram-pushers and wheelchair users. A gate system with push-button control was used for a while, but it was obvious something more radical was needed for pedestrians to negotiate the increasingly hectic junction.

And so, at great expense, came the subway. In the late 1960s, the council decided that since crossing the A5103 either on the same level as, or above, the traffic was problematic or dangerous, the only other solution was to take pedestrians underground. I remember well those echoing, freezing, rain-swept and slightly sinister yellow canyons of the infamous Northenden underpass. There were tales of mugging and worse going on down there. I don't know about that, but my lasting memory is of the graffiti.

In a future century, some team on an archaeological dig will uncover the walls of that partially subterranean warren, which was filled in at even greater expense in 1988. If the indelible black paint has survived, they will find daubed along one stretch the following, in neatly turned, foot-high letters:

Ziggy Stardust Aladdin Sane
He changes his face along with
  his name
But whatever his make-up
His cause we will take up
And join in each verse with refrain.

I wonder what that future generation will make of it?

Pedestrians now cross safely at the lights, under the imposing flyover. The express north-south traffic flows unimpeded, and you can walk from Palatine Road to Wythenshawe Road – or vice versa – without anything too exciting happening to you.

ON THE CURRY MILE

One of the free delights of South Manchester, especially on a warm summer's evening, is a stroll down Wilmslow Road in Rusholme, sampling the smells and sights of the Curry Mile.

Now with its own council-financed direction signs and near-international fame, the Mile (actually just over half that distance) is the city's cultural and commercial phenomenon of the last thirty years.

The original Asian restaurant in Rusholme is generally accepted to be the New Taj Mahal, which opened in 1959, although around that time there were other similar establishments in Manchester, especially on Upper Brook Street and Levenshulme's Stockport Road. Later 'superb curries and Indian meals' were advertised at the short-lived Padna Indian restaurant at 682 Burnage Lane in Didsbury – now the Tondori Royale.

But in Rusholme – as yet – very little. The New Taj Mahal seems to

An artist's impression of the first Rusholme curry house,
based on the 1959 photograph. (Phil Blinston)

have disappeared fairly quickly. The row of shops and cafés was demolished in the late 1960s, and the address is now occupied by the Shere Khan restaurant. A more permanent fixture was the Raj Mahal ('select Indian and English meals') down the road at no. 40, roughly where the Al-Safa Tandoori takeaway is now. This establishment lasted the decade, as did the larger Jalalabad at no. 152, whose owners astutely added a coffee bar and licensed casino to the dining-out facilities. That establishment too is now long gone. There is now a row of townhouses on the site, opposite Rusholme Grove.

As accurately observed in BBC One's *Life on Mars*, the Mile in the early 1970s was still predominantly English shops, with the odd curry house a novelty item. Throughout that decade, the Asian influence grew, so that, by the mid-1980s, the original

5 per cent of Asians on the Mile had rocketed to around 95 per cent. The success of one business, whether restaurant, jewellers or clothing shop, had attracted others. On one central row a fishmonger, an ironmonger, a branch of the Royal Bank of Scotland, and the Trocadero cinema had all disappeared by the 1990s, to be replaced by Asian businesses.

The changes can be roughly followed by looking at one address: no. 119 Wilmslow Road (near to Thurloe Street). This was originally Seymour Mead's grocers in the early twentieth century. By the mid-1960s, it was owned by Rusholme Light Car Co., before being taken over by the Shezan restaurateurs in 1976. It remained in business until 2003, and is now the Marrakesh Shisha Café, reflecting the current widening popularity of the hookah in multicultural Manchester.

The person to ask about the last forty years on the Mile is Abdul Qayyum, co-owner of the Sanam. This is the restaurant that has lasted the longest, maintaining its premises and its popularity from its foundation in 1968 until the present day. Mr Qayyum takes pride in the fact that customers have included professional footballers, most of the *Coronation Street* cast, and Simply Red's Mick Hucknall. Famous boxers have shown a liking for the Sanam: memorably Mike Tyson, Prince Naseem, and Amir Khan. Muhammad Ali came in one Sunday morning looking for a halal breakfast.

The Mile is at its most spectacular during the festival of Eid, which celebrates the end of the Ramadan fasting, and which acts as a magnet for revellers across Greater Manchester. Wilmslow Road on that warm and spicy summer night becomes a vividly lit concourse, loud with blaring horns, where the occasional stretch limo tries to edge its way through the crush of strolling crowds, and close-packed groups of impromptu dancers leap to drums and tambourines.

The contrast with the Rusholme of the 1960s, with the rows of traditional English shops, cafés and the odd launderette or garage, could hardly be more pronounced.

SIX

SPORTING LIVES

BRIGADIER'S BIG DAY

Down Burton Road in Withington, opposite where the swimming baths are now, there used to be a pub known as the Waterloo Hotel. The site is now occupied by a new development: Brigadier Close. And thereby hangs a tale.

One day in the mid-1860s, the pub owner, one William Foulkes, picked up a stray dog. The greyhound, given the name Brigadier, turned out to be a lucrative investment for all concerned. He was trained by a Mr Gorton, and entered for the prestigious Waterloo Cup – the 'Blue Riband of the Leash' – in February 1866.

The Waterloo Cup was a money-laden championship of the now banned sport of hare coursing.

Sixty-four greyhounds or dogs of similar hunting breed were paired off to race against each other, and the three-day-long event continued on a knock-out basis, until one dog was proclaimed champion.

The venue was usually in the flat and parcelled farmland around Great Altcar, Sefton, in what is now Merseyside. A different field would be used for each day's competition, which would begin around 10 a.m. with a line of beaters driving a hare into the event field. What the hare's thoughts were on being dragged from his winter lie-in and forced into an open space full of roaring humans and a couple of enthusiastic and slavering high-speed predators are perhaps best left unrecorded.

In the interests of fairness, the hare was given a start of around 100 yards before a neutral steward, known as the slipper, unleashed the dogs simultaneously. It was rare that the quarry was actually caught, and the dogs were awarded points for speed and how many times they forced the hare to change direction. There were plenty of escape routes from the event area, and once the target Lepus had managed to elude his pursuers, the beaters set about driving another hare (or – depressing thought – the same one again) into the field, for the next pair of dogs.

There was big money riding on an ultimate win, with a prize fund of 1,000 sovereigns – about a quarter of a million pounds in today's money.

Highly regarded was Isaac, owned by a Mr Brocklebank. Early odds quoted him at 12-1, with Brigadier an outsider at 50-1. After the first day's competition, Brigadier's win over the more experienced Naworth shortened his odds to 30-1. The next day began with a relatively easy defeat of the unfancied Heroic, which put the Withington dog into the last 16. Later that day, another win saw Brigadier reach the quarter-final, with his odds shortening to 8-1. Isaac was still clear favourite on 7-2, while the smart money was being drawn towards Fieldfare (8-1), a newcomer like Brigadier, so a bit of an unknown quantity.

Finals day started with a couple of shocks: Isaac was beaten, and second favourite Lady Alexander lost to Fieldfare. Brigadier had the easiest route to the semi, outrunning 100-8 shot Belle of the Cottage. Third favourite, Theatre Royal, was dismissed in the semi-final, which led to a final 'deciding course' against bookies' favourite Fieldfare.

Amidst great excitement, Brigadier proved himself faster and more efficient than his adversary, winning the trophy and making his owner and trainer very rich men.

Brigadier no doubt dined on steak for the rest of his days. He died in 1877, aged 14, and was buried in a grave with a headstone in the grounds of the Waterloo Inn. The grave disappeared along with the inn, but a plaque on the wall at the entrance to Brigadier Close keeps his memory alive today.

Champion greyhound Brigadier's grave in the grounds of the Waterloo Inn, Withington.

THE DAY OF THE AMATEUR

As the manic whine of the World Cup vuvuzelas recedes mercifully into the past, and as yet another domestic footie season gets underway, please bear with me for a while as I stay with soccer, but shift the focus.

A hundred years or so ago, amateur football in England was a far slicker and more powerful animal than it is today. Many of the players in the full England international team were amateurs. With the maximum soccer wage stuck at £4 a week, there was no great incentive for a footballer who earned his living elsewhere to join the professional ranks. University sides were still redoubtable opponents who could often hold their own against the top League clubs.

So when a team from Chorlton-cum-Hardy reached the semi-final of the 1907 Lancashire Amateur Cup, this was recognised as an impressive achievement. They beat local rivals Whalley Range 3-1, and won the right to travel to Lancaster to take on the strong Manchester University team in the final.

The University, having scored over a hundred goals that season, were favourites to win. However, on a day of heavy rain and high wind, the Chorlton side surprised the pundits by adapting better to the conditions and defeating their fancied opponents by a single goal: 'a thundering half-volley that gave the keeper no chance'. Soccer took root in the township that had been newly incorporated into the City of Manchester.

The early years of the twentieth century saw the appearance in the area of several football clubs, some of them short-lived: Chorlton Albion (1925), whose home pitch was on the corner of Hardy Lane and Barlow Moor Road, near to where the Co-op is now; Chorlton Amateurs (1921), who played off Egerton Road North, near the railway line; Chorltonville (1924), who had a pitch off Hampton Road, near to Longford Park; Chorlton Road Congregation (1911-14), who played on a pitch off Elsinore Road, Old Trafford.

A couple of clubs lasted the course, with spectacular results. East Chorlton FC were, for many years, one of the strongest amateur sides in the north-west. Originally calling themselves Wilbrampton (presumably a coinage from Wilbraham and Chorlton), their early homes in the 1930s were Withington Road, then the Boat House Field in Northenden. Their glory years, in which they won every available trophy, came when their home pitch was on the sodden, rain-lashed open space of Hough End. After shifting their home venue to the Brookburn Road pitch on the Meadows (now West Didsbury and Chorlton FC's ground) their fortunes went into a decline, and they folded in 1994.

Still alive and kicking, however, are Chorltonians, formed in 1928 by some old boys of Chorlton High School under the aegis of Headmaster Alf Chappell. Their original name of Old Chorltonians lasted until 2007, when they dropped the 'Old'.

A full history of the club is on their excellent website. Now the area's flag-ship soccer outfit is popular enough to run six teams, of whom the first XI brought the prestigious Rhodes Cup back to Chorlton in 2010. They were then Lancashire and Cheshire Amateur League Champions the fol-lowing season. Their home venue is the Greater Manchester Police sta-dium on Hough End, a few hundred yards away from the High School where it all began.

WIMBLEDON ON PALATINE ROAD

The Northern Tennis Club in West Didsbury had been in use for just over a year in 1910. Before that, since 1882, the Northern had had its home at Old Trafford, just across the railway line from the Lancashire cricket ground, and down the road from what was to become the Manchester United stadium. One of the approaches was along Tennis Street, a minor thoroughfare which still exists, just off Seymour Grove. Wimbledon stars who played there

Mrs Ethel Larcombe, Wimbledon Ladies' Champion, about to serve at the Northern Tennis Club in West Didsbury in 1910. (Northern Lawn Tennis Club)

during the late nineteenth century were Herbert Wilberforce (great-grandson of the campaigner against slavery), seven times Men's Singles Champion William Renshaw, Reggie Doherty, and Dr W.V. Eaves. In 1882, the Northern was the first tennis club to introduce Ladies' Tournaments, two years before Wimbledon.

In those mid-Victorian days the Old Trafford home had been ideal. Trafford Park was indeed a park, with the verdant wooded grounds of the de Trafford estate, where herds of fallow deer roamed free, sweep-ing away to the south and west.

Sir Humphrey de Trafford was the club's first President.

And then came the Ship Canal, and massive industrialisation. Within twenty-five years the sylvan Eden was transformed into Coketown, as Trafford Park became the largest industrial estate in Europe. Smoke belched from factory and mill chimneys and frequently passing trains. The club secretary recorded: 'During the later years at Old Trafford, new balls became black after only a few games, and a collision with the stop-netting caused a well-defined pattern of it to appear on one's flannels.'

The move to West Didsbury was a perfect solution. It was a smart residential area with a railway station just down the lane, and a good volley's distance from green farmland. The attractive half-timbered pavilion at Old Trafford, too iconic and eye-catching to leave behind, was dismantled and reassembled at the new site.

The big names still came, and squash and croquet were added to the hive of sporting activity. The only times that the Northern has lain fallow was during the two world wars. In the Second World War horses and donkeys grazed on the lush grass, and the groundsman later recalled clearing the courts of anti-aircraft shrapnel before mowing them. A weekly class for club juniors was the only tennis interest.

The list of household names who have played at the Northern over the past forty years or so makes impressive reading: Billie-Jean King, Evonne Cawley, Jimmy Connors, Virginia Wade, Stan Smith, Ken Rosewall, Sue Barker, Roscoe Tanner, John McEnroe, Pat Rafter, Stefan Edberg, Pete Sampras, Goran Ivanošević … it's like a Who's Who of tennis.

Didsbury has hosted several Davis Cup matches, and until 1982 was the home of the official pre-Wimbledon tournament.

The club continues to introduce youngsters to tennis. Coaching sessions for children aged from five to sixteen are organised during the summer holidays. Transport, refreshments, and a free ticket to the Manchester Trophy are provided.

The Northern will figure significantly in the 2012 Olympics, as its splendid grass courts, still amongst the finest in the UK, will be in demand as training facilities for visiting countries.

CITY'S CRAZY SEASON

The two Manchester football teams slugging it out in the Premiership might bring to mind a crunch match between the same two teams, in the FA Cup this time, all of eighty-six years ago.

FIFA had just changed the offside rule, making it much easier to score if you were a nippy enough forward. So goals were pouring in – at both ends. The 1925/6 League season could only have happened to City: a rich harvest of eighty-nine goals scored, but a round 100 let in. They were relegated.

However, again essential City, they also reached the Cup Final in the same season, netting thirty-one goals in six games. After a 3-3 draw in the Third Round with amateur cream the Corinthians, the replay was held at Maine Road, City's new home for just three years. The result was a hearty 4-0 win for the Manchester side. Next were reigning League Champions Huddersfield Town. Another 4-0 drubbing ensued.

Top strikers were centre-forward Frank Roberts (four England caps), Tommy Browell, the inside-left with his trademark air-to-ground headers, and left-winger George Hicks, slight of build but a mercurial dribbler.

Crystal Palace of the old Third Division South were the opponents in the Fifth Round. Whilst a fairly straightforward win for the top flight club was predicted, the outlandish scoreline wasn't. The first half was all City: seven goals without reply. Then in a twenty minute spell in the second half the Palace turned the game on its head, achieving a 4-1 in their favour. The blues finished with a three-goal flourish to win 11-4, creating what the *Manchester Guardian* called 'a lacrosse score'. For a reason no

longer apparent, the Palace fans carried their goalkeeper off the pitch shoulder-high at the end.

Clapton Orient, away, were considered tougher opponents in the quarter-final, but the Manchester men rolled on, dismissing the Londoners 6-1 with a display of 'disciplined cleverness', according to the *Athletic News.*

Next was that semi with United, played at Bramall Lane, Sheffield. United's season so far had had its own share of ups and downs. City had beaten them 6-1 at Old Trafford, but United's League form generally had been superior. In the Cup, United had already ousted Spurs and Sunderland, but a sluggish defence and wrong choice of attacking strategy let them down on the day. The Maine Road men triumphed 3-0, in front of a crowd of 45,500.

The Final at Wembley was against Bolton Wanderers, who had won the Cup three years previously, with virtually the same team. Unsurprisingly, it was the Wanderers who settled more quickly to the task, whilst City's nerves, after all that business with the brass bands, community singing, and shaking hands with King George, were hampering their usual free-flowing attacks. Bolton scored the vital goal, and City had to wait another eight years before lifting the trophy. Within a week they were in Division Two – but they'd be back.

SUNNY LOWRY – CHANNEL SWIMMER

When 15-year-old Ethel 'Sunny' Lowry was asked by her Headmistress at Manchester High School for Girls what her ambition in life was, the reply was given with no hesitation: 'To swim the Channel.' The Headmistress's response was equally succinct: 'Dismissed.'

Fortunately, Sunny Lowry from Rusholme was too much her own person to be turned aside by official indifference. A member of Victoria Baths Ladies, she had already won prizes for long-distance swimming, notably at Lake Windermere.

Six years later, coach Jabez Wolffe was looking for a likely protégé to take on the Channel swim. Wolffe himself had made twenty-two attempts, but despite some near-misses, had never succeeded. Sunny was selected out of 300 applicants, and training began.

Coach and swimmer set up camp at Westgate-on-Sea, near Margate. Now swimming for three to four hours a day, and undergoing gym sessions with a medicine ball, Sunny was put on Wolffe's secret weapon – a high-protein diet. This meant eggs – eight of which went into a daily breakfast omelette.

Sunny's first attempt to swim the Channel was made on 10 August 1932. She entered the water at Shakespeare Cliffs at 4.45 p.m., watched by a crowd of around 3,000. The overnight section saw Sunny dealing with a belt of seaweed, and overcoming the swell from the passing mail boat. At dawn, with the lights of Calais visible, the sea became choppy and a bitterly cold headwind arose. A feeble sun shone through, but in the end the black and freezing water took its toll, and the attempt had to be abandoned with just four miles to go.

Ethel 'Sunny' Lowry (1911-2008), Channel swimmer. (Diane Inglis and Jill Cronin)

Sunny was undaunted: 'I'll be back for vengeance on Old Man Channel.'

One year on, in July 1933, Lowry was back in the water, fitter and better prepared. Starting out from Cap Gris Nez this time, in ideal conditions and with a gentle breeze behind her, she covered the first half of the journey in a phenomenal 5½ hours. At this rate, every record in the book would be smashed.

Then, at 1.15 a.m., there was a distant rumble of thunder. Within minutes the wind switched direction and rose to a howling gale, and in the violent thunderstorm waves started to crash over the deck of the accompanying tug. Sunny's red cap was intermittently visible in the flashes of forked lightning, but it took some time to locate her and haul her aboard. Continuing in these conditions was obviously out of the question, yet a sobbing Sunny pleaded to be allowed to continue.

Old Man Channel had won again, but he was up against a formidable adversary. One month later, on 28 August, Lowry was having another go, starting out from Cap Gris Nez once more, and this time covering the first half in a mind-boggling four hours. At one point during the night a shoal of jellyfish, usually a potential hazard with their stings, surrounded her, as if accompanying her progress, dolphin-like. It was an omen: despite adverse currents in the last mile, Sunny reached the beach at St Margaret's Bay, cheered on by holidaymakers, at 10.30 a.m.

The news was telegrammed to Manchester, where Sunny's father, who worked as a fish wholesaler at Shudehill market, led a celebratory dance around the stalls.

Ethel Lowry was awarded the MBE in 2005, was elected President of the Channel Swimming Association, and was instrumental in the campaign to restore Victoria Baths. Her story now features in the International Maritime Hall of Fame in Fort Lauderdale.

SEVEN

READ ALL ABOUT IT

THE SOUTH MANCHESTER GAZETTE

The *South Manchester Gazette* was a weekly eight-page broadsheet which covered roughly the same area the *South Manchester Reporter* does today. It came out on Saturday mornings, cost one old penny, and was so popular that the first issue in May 1885 had sold out before 9 a.m.!

It was great value for a penny, and it's still a rattling good read more than 125 years on. The format was usually the same: the front page was given over to corporate adverts and announcements of local or general interest (the opening of Rusholme Baths, tricycle hire in Fallowfield, where to go if you wanted to make a phone call, have your house decorated, or get your plumbing fixed, the latest in false teeth or wonder hair restorer, etc.), then a section on international and national news, followed by local items divided up into districts. Sport was well catered for: Association and Rugby Football, cycling, cricket, lacrosse, bowls and rounders all figured.

The back page had the small ads, such as 'Situations Vacant' and 'For Sale'. A perambulator and a banjo were up for grabs in the first issue, and the following reflects the mostly rural aspect of the newspaper's catchment area:

FOR SALE: a good, useful GREY MARE (aged). Suit farmer for breeding, ploughing or cart. Apply JAS. BERRY & SONS, Nurserymen, Alexandra Park.

The regular features are also interesting. There was a whole weekly column devoted to 'Something for the

West Didsbury shops on Barlow Moor Road, *c.* 1900. John Tripp's post office and general stores (on the site of what is now The Flower Lounge) was one of the many sales outlets for the *South Manchester Gazette*. (Manchester Central Library Local Image Collection: ref.m21228)

Young', which contained educational snippets, short adventure stories, and a series of puzzles, or 'nuts to crack'. Try this one (solution at the end):

I consist of ten letters.
My 3, 5, 10, 7 is part of a ship.
My 9, 5, 7 is a quadruped.
My 3, 5, 4 is a biped.
My whole represents a healthy
pastime.

Other features included the following:

'Comic Cuts': although the Victorian enthusiasm for puns would probably not be fully shared today: 'The most popular opera-glasses – those between the acts.'

'Facts and Fancies': new scientific ideas, oddball news items from around the world.

'Bits from books': extracts from contemporary best sellers: mostly adventure, comedy, or self-help tracts.

'Hints for the home': although not billed as such, this was the women's section, with such domestic items as how to cook macaroni, shift those stubborn stains, or attract a better class of husband. The role of women in mid-Victorian society was usually

Front page of the *South Manchester Gazette*, 27 June 1885.

well defined: 'A wife should be like roast lamb, tender and nicely dressed. No sauce required.' If that made your hackles rise, try this, from the same column a month or so later: 'A woman may be loved for her superior intellect, a love serious but rare.'

Hang on to your monocles, chaps, here come the suffragettes.

Solution to puzzle: GYMNASTICS.

GREEN ISSUES

Way back in the 1980s there appeared the monthly publication *Chorlton Green*, a cheap (15p) and cheerful alternative newspaper. It was typed and photocopied – none of your fancy modern-day desktop publishing – onto A4 sheets, 12 or 16 pages per issue. Its mission, veering left of centre, was to 'offer Chorlton the voice it's never had before – in personal opinion, in creative work, and as an information exchange.'

Financed by adverts from local shops and businesses, it ran for just over two years. Despite its short lifespan and erratic appearances, *Chorlton Green* can claim to have had a significant influence on the cultural life of the suburb.

The April 1984 issue posed the question: 'Why is there such a dearth of community arts activity in our area?' This seems harsh, as South Manchester at the time was far from the implied cultural desert. Perhaps what was lacking was the networking. A meeting organised by the newspaper led to the Summer Festival in August of that year, at which, besides the stalls, face-painting and bouncy castle, Chorlton Park was treated to the sights and sounds of alternative theatre groups and blues and rock bands. The origins of the annual Arts Festival can be traced to this initiative.

Public views were sought on how the area could be improved. The expressed needs were: a theatre, a film club, more restaurants and a wine bar, improved swimming baths, and a live music venue. Interestingly, given a recent well-publicised local difference of opinion (the 2009 dispute over whether to build soccer pitches on part of Chorlton Meadows; the conservationists won the day), sports buffs were asking for 'more football pitches, especially 5-a-side'.

The creative part of the editorial pledge was satisfied by publication of readers' photographs, and a poets' corner. Memorable was Alex Hamilton's 'Ode to a Pint', with its nod to Robbie Burns:

Great tawny, frothy, sparkling beaker
O, there's such beauty in thy features ...

Adverts from days gone by included the Aaben cinema, the Beech Road bookshop, Bridge Shoe Repairs, the Army and Navy Stores, and The Gym (now Bodyshapers) on Albany Road. Remember them? And did anybody avail themselves of the services of Livewires Singing Telegrams?

The newspaper's focus often shifted further out from the parochial. Hollywood film star Jean Simmons, in town filming for a Granada TV play, was spotted and photographed: 'Green Scoops Jean' boasted the headline. Cosgrove Hall's BAFTA award for *The Wind in the Willows* (see page 126) received suitable front-page coverage. The Greenham Common debate came home to Beech Road, where a temporary peace camp in the park received some stick, including some verbal vitriol from a councillor.

Such unpleasantness was a rarity in the publica,tion's pages. The generally light-hearted tone included some gently satirical cartoons. In one, a dungaree-clad woman sporting a CND badge is consoling her similarly dressed friend: 'Don't worry, Mr Left will come along one day.'

Star of the September 1984 issue has to be Stuart Holmes, Chorlton's one-man anti-smoking campaign. He pedalled his eye-catching vehicle – a composite of pushbike, pram and advertising hoardings – from place to place, spreading the word of abstinence from the weed. It just goes to show: it may take a while, but the lone and sincere voice tends to get itself heard.

EIGHT

A MUSICAL INTERLUDE

ON A CAROUSEL

According to Wikipedia and its off-shoots, and at least 50 per cent of Merseysiders, the iconic Liverpool FC song 'You'll Never Walk Alone' (YNWA) was first delivered by a football crowd at Anfield in November 1963.

However, new and existing evidence suggests strongly that the received wisdom on the subject is incorrect. It's looking now as if Manchester United fans – at least, a few of them – beat the Kop to it by five and a half years.

Let's put aside for the moment any knee-jerk reactions, and consider some oft-quoted assertions:

Liverpudlian pop singer Gerry Marsden wrote the song 'You'll Never Walk Alone' in 1963.

No, he didn't. The Rodgers and Hammerstein song was first performed as part of the Broadway show *Carousel* in 1945.

Gerry and the Pacemakers' 1963 recording was the first popular mainstream version of the song released.

Not if you include earlier versions by Frank Sinatra (1945), Judy Garland (1945), Louis Armstrong (1954), Mario Lanza (1952 and 1956), Perry Como (1956), Gene Vincent (1957), Nina Simone (1959), and Doris Day (1962), amongst others. The album of the *Carousel* film soundtrack was in the LP charts for over a year in the mid-1950s, and reached no. 26 in the *singles* charts.

Liverpool fans were the first to adopt the song as their anthem, and over the years have been by far the most consistent and enthusiastic singers en masse.

Unarguably. The evidence is over-whelming. Examples of archive film, and cultural and media references, are legion. Already by the 1965 FA Cup Final, commentator Kenneth Wolstenholme referred to the song as 'the Liverpool signature tune'. In the nation's eyes, the club-song link was intensified after the Hillsborough disaster of 1989.

> Mario Lanza sang the song at Old Trafford soon after the Munich air crash in 1958.

Untrue. Mario Lanza never performed at Old Trafford football ground, and his repertoire at King's Hall, Belle Vue, Manchester on 6 March 1958 didn't even include YNWA.

> Chorlton-cum-Hardy Operatic Society were rehearsing 'Carousel' in around 1960, and several of their members sang the song at Old Trafford.

Easy to dismiss. Chorlton-cum-Hardy Operatic Society, founded in 1907, didn't even exist in the 1950s and '60s.

> The song was sung by a section of the Old Trafford crowd at the first match following the Munich air dis-aster in February 1958.

This has always been at the very least plausible, and, it would now appear, is true. Major, but not the only, source for this is Jane Hardwick, former member of the New Mills Operatic Society, who was present at the match in question: the FA Cup tie with Sheffield Wednesday. She has given me permission to quote extracts from her emails to me on the subject:

> I know and accept that it is now Liverpool's anthem and always will be, that is beyond doubt. It became their song after Gerry and the Pacemakers made it a hit and I, for one, am more than happy to acknowledge this fact. When you hear the song you think of Liverpool FC quite naturally and I would never wish to detract from that.
>
> However, at the end of the day 'You'll Never Walk Alone' was sung by me and my friends (in floods of tears) at Old Trafford soon after the Munich disaster ...
>
> The film Carousel was extremely popular at the time, therefore many people were aware of the song. We stood on the 'popular' side for all home matches. There were proba-bly 8-10 of us, mainly boys and just 2 or 3 girls (not all of us from the New Mills Operatic Society) who travelled by train from New Mills. We met up with about 15 other fans who regularly stood near us for the matches ...
>
> I have spoken to my brother, and he agrees that the song was sung during the first home match after the crash when the programme had the United team selection completely blank ... [This would be the FA Cup match *v*. Sheffield Wednesday on 19 February 1958.]

I remember my parents remarking on it when I saw them back home. They had HEARD the singing from the opposite side of the ground.

So why haven't more people come forward to corroborate the claim? One has. I spoke to a Chorlton lady, a well-respected local historian and church archivist who was in the Stretford End crowd at Old Trafford on 19 February 1958. She recalled the following, incidentally without any prompting or interruptions from me:

(1) 'You'll Never Walk Alone' was definitely sung at the FA Cup tie with Sheffield Wednesday, the first home match after Munich.
(2) The singing started on the popular side (the eastern side of the ground).
(3) It was clearly audible on the Stretford End (the southern side).
(4) At least a thousand people joined in (which is credible, since, according to Jane Hardwick, the singing was also heard on the main stand on the opposite side to the popular terraces).

The details tally so closely with those given by Jane Hardwick (whom the lady has never met or spoken to) that any impartial historian will concede that the Old Trafford claim now has to be taken seriously.

But why has only one person backed up the claim?

How many people can recall what was being sung at a specific football match over fifty years ago – even assuming they're still around? Bear in mind that in 1958, 'You'll Never Walk Alone' was just another song, yet to be loaded with the pronounced Liverpool associations, and therefore not particularly noteworthy or memorable. Which is, incidentally, why you won't find any reference to the singing in any contemporary newspaper report of the Old Trafford match: at the time it wasn't considered worth a mention. Jane Hardwick remembers it, as she started the singing!

In conclusion, as an unbiased football and local historian I have to say that the evidence is strong enough to support the view that 'You'll Never Walk Alone' was indeed sung by a section of the Man United crowd at Old Trafford in February 1958. Doubtless I will get verbally lashed by Liverpool fans or those of a stubborn mind-set, but if so, my response would be, in the words of Isaac Newton: 'I have studied it. You have not.'

THE GOSPEL TRUTH

In May 1964, when the pop charts were firmly in the grip of the Mersey Sound, there was a concert at the Free Trade Hall, Manchester, featuring some of the top names in US

Blues and Gospel. It was part of a British tour, and involved, amongst others, Muddy Waters, Sister Rosetta Tharpe, Brownie McGhee, and Cousin Joe Pleasant.

It was a rare gathering of talent, and Granada TV Producer John Hamp, thinking brilliantly outside the box, as it were, dreamed up the idea of the Blues and Gospel Train.

The disused Wilbraham Road station in Whalley Range underwent a glorious one-off makeover. Devouring the whole budget, seventy staff transformed the station into a slice of deep Dixie: sawdust, crates, WANTED posters, a rocking chair, milk churns, convincing clapboard and shutters, and the odd goat and puzzled chicken strolling around.

The sign said 'Chorltonville', which has led to the myth that all this took place on the site of the new Metrolink station by Morrison's in Chorlton. This wasn't the case: the flyer advertising the event ('casual gear essential') states: 'Entrance to the station is in Athol Road'.

Most of the fans arrived by train, of course, catching the 7.30 special from Central Station (now the G-Mex). This was the night before the Free Trade Hall concert, so it gave the performers a chance of a relatively relaxed dress rehearsal for the main event.

Any showbiz person will tell you that entrances are important. Putting the new radio microphone to good use, here were two classics. First Muddy Waters strolled in along the track with his suitcase and downcast face, playing the pilgrim hobo with his world-weary philosophy: 'You Can't Lose What You Ain't Never Had', sung in that melancholy, savvy voice that felt like velvet running through gravel.

Sister Rosetta's entrance was more upmarket. A one-horse carriage and a regal walk brought her to the platform, where she sang 'Didn't It Rain?' (It did, too.) There was something about that delivery and phrasing: close your eyes and deepen the voice, and there was bluesy Elvis. Then she launched into a spellbinding Gibson guitar solo, after which she couldn't resist saying, 'Not bad for a woman, eh?'

On piano was Cousin Joe Pleasant. He was the one who, in the face of initial scepticism from his co-performers, had held fast to the idea of the UK and European tour, ultimately ensuring it took place. If you ever need cheering up, find Cousin Joe's rendition of the hilarious 'Hot Dog' on YouTube, taken from this very Blues and Gospel Train concert. It's a send-up of a traditional twelve-bar blues, with the piano variations scampering around it like a frisky dog.

Amongst the other performers, of interest is the inscrutable bassist Ransom Knowling, who was almost a permanent fixture as a session musician on many rock'n'roll standards in the early '60s.

The whole event was filmed, and selected highlights appeared in a

Granada TV programme the following August. With perhaps an impish touch from the programme planners, it was screened midweek at 9.40 p.m., immediately after a Conservative Party political broadcast!

Thankfully, the internet has preserved many of these highlights. Listen to the performances now and you can hear the approaching styles of Chuck Berry, Elvis and his many imitators, Aretha Franklin, the Stones, Fleetwood Mac, and other icons of mainstream pop. It's a precious piece of musical history, and it all happened one rainy May evening in South Manchester, nearly fifty years ago.

BEYOND THE VALLEY OF THE PUNKS

When punk rock first crashed onto the British pop scene some thirty-five years ago, at first it was a breath of fresh air, a loud and welcome raspberry aimed at the complacent sweetness of a glam-pop establishment that had lost its edge along with most of its talent.

But as soon as punk started to take itself seriously – from the moment that it styled itself as a movement – it became in its turn ripe for the picking.

Enter Alberto y Lost Trios Paranoias, or 'The Berts' for short. Originally a comedy outfit that mutated from South Manchester hippy band Greasy Bear, it grew in numbers and widened its purpose in 1974, and was soon on the same bill as the likes of Hawkwind, Blondie, the Stranglers and the Police. Lead vocals were shared between Chris 'CP' Lee, Bob Harding, Jimmy Hibbert and the late Les Prior. There was former Greasy Bear drummer Bruce Mitchell, guitarists Simon White and Tony Bowers, and another drummer in the person of Ray 'Mighty Mongo' Hughes. It was an impressive array of musical talent, and all of the gang hailed from South Manchester.

The Barron-Knights and the Bonzo Dogs had been lampooning popular music for a while, but under the influence of The Berts the posturing underwent another turn of the satirical screw.

The entire culture of the repetitive strain injury riff (Status Quo for starters) was sent up with the joyous 'Heads Down No-nonsense Mindless Boogie', with its addictive five-note musical phrase and recommendation: 'Bang your 'ead on the wall'. This one actually made the charts: no. 28 in 1978.

But enough of easy targets: under the withering attention of The Berts no icon was left unstoned. Lou Reed's 'Heroin' was re-cast as 'Anadin', complete with dark glasses and fake vomit. The smoochy

Alberto y Lost Trios Paranoias, or the Berts for short. (C.P. Lee)

Aznavour-style love song was deconstructed into French phrase book drills. The pretend death cult, supposedly haunting punk's outer limits, was shown in its true colours of commercially viable emo pose. The musical play 'Snuff Rock' did for punk what Rocky Horror did for body-building courses.

The normal concert parameters became an irrelevance. A mock fight left one of the guitarists flat out on the stage, where he remained for most of the performance. Two vocalists would launch into different songs, each apparently oblivious of the other. A succession of gig saboteurs, with everything from a vampire bat to a cartoon bomb, was absorbed into the anarchy. A band member inexplicably holding aloft an ice cream throughout the show morphed into the Statue of Liberty at the curtain call.

The band's name was a play on Alberto y los Trios Paraguayos, a Latin American ensemble who had enjoyed a middle of the road popularity since the 1950s. Did anybody ever go to a concert of The Berts expecting to hear Guantanamera and La Bamba?

Ideas thought up in the van trips between shows formed the basis of the carefully choreographed and orchestrated lunacy on stage. For most of the 1970s The Berts were in demand, performing at venues across the UK and Europe, and taking 'Snuff Rock' to New York. When asked which gig stands out as special in his memory, Didsbury ex-member Chris Lee plumps for the Free Trade Hall, Manchester. I never had the chance to see the group live, but their musical antics are fondly remembered by a generation of Mancunians.

NINE

FIRE AND WATER

FIRES IN THE NIGHT

At 1.40 a.m. on Sunday, 12 November 1899, Withington Town Hall received a phone call informing them of a building on fire near Northenden Bridge. It turned out to be the Grand Pavilion Refreshment House, a high-class temperance establishment run by Frenchman Constantine Logios and his wife. It was thought that a gas explosion in the kitchen had started the blaze.

This being several decades before the 999 facility was introduced, and given that few dwellings were in 'telephonic communication', the emergency wheels were comparatively slow to grind into motion.

The phone call was relayed to the Manchester Fire Station on Jackson's Row, and an engine was duly sent out. The fire by now was a substantial one, visible across the fields as far north as Dickenson Road. Two fire engines, one from Jackson's Row and another from Chorlton-on-Medlock, raced down Palatine Road as far as the Mersey Bridge, which in those days marked the boundary with Cheshire.

Here the story meets with a stunning display of red tape inertia. Having established that the fire was 50 yards across the border, and that no lives were at risk, the firemen refused to venture beyond the bridge, and as the flames lit up the night sky, turned around and went home.

It was up to a local resident to cycle the three miles to Sale, from where another fire engine was sent. However, by the time it arrived, the Grand Pavilion Refreshment House had burned to the ground.

Despite the fact that the building had only been partly insured, phoenix-like it rose again bigger and better, now an imposing two-storey café, restaurant and hotel that continued to meet the teetotal and gastronomic demands of the more well-off locals.

Monsieur Logios also organised dances, at which the intention was to teach the villagers how to waltz. Unfortunately, the sessions proved none-too-popular.

Otherwise, for the next five years, the re-named Pavilion Café flourished. Then, perhaps spookily, almost exactly five years later, once more at around 1 a.m., it caught fire again.

They say lightning never strikes the same place twice, which is why it's usually at this point that conspiracy theorists start to form a scrum: Arson out of pure malice or devilment? Anti-temperance feelings running high? Racism against a foreign interloper? An insurance scam? Or just another accident with the gas?

At this distance in time, it's impossible to say for sure what caused the second Pavilion fire, but on this occasion the story unfolded differently. Perhaps remembering the jobsworth inactivity of five years before, local hero John Baines, who lived on Mill Lane, hopped on his bike and once more pedalled up to Sale.

The Sale fire station was behind the Town Hall, where the library is now. There were stables opposite, so horses were available, but Superintendent Hunt opted for the steam-powered machine. Slow to start, and operating on the same principle as the steam railway engine with on-board coal supply, the vehicle could reach a nippy 40mph once under way.

This time the fire brigade arrived early enough to save a large proportion of the Café from the flames. Nevertheless, damage was estimated to have run into hundreds of pounds, which translates into a modern-day six-figure sum.

Monsieur Logios, whose wife had died three years earlier, committed suicide by shooting himself. There is no building on the site on the 1906 OS map. Nowadays the site is occupied by the three-storey flats beside St Hilda's Close, Northenden.

There is an eerie postscript: Winifred Garner, whilst researching her 1986 book on Northenden history, spoke to a lady who had decided not to take one of the rear flats, as she had felt 'a distant air of tragedy which depressed her.' The lady asked if anything tragic had occurred there in the past. (Thanks for information supplied by K.C. Hawker of Northenden.)

The remains of Monsieur Logios's hotel-restaurant after the second fire. (Northenden Civic Society)

EARTHQUAKE AND FLOODS

As we cursed the arctic weather last winter, perhaps the world news brought it home to us that as far as weather extremes and natural disasters go, we have it cushy. We see the devastation wreaked by earthquakes and tsunamis, and realise that what makes local front page news and is a cause for a moan back home would simply raise a smile (or a bitter laugh) in less temperate regions of the world. What's 'extreme' for us is small beer elsewhere.

Do you remember 19 July 1984? The largest onshore earthquake in British history grumbled into life on the Llyn Peninsula, North Wales. Two adjoining subterranean plates of rock, having rubbed each other up the wrong way, had finally had enough of each other's proximity and fallen out, big time. Earthly shudders spread as far as Scarborough, London, Newcastle, and Dublin. South Manchester was well within the area affected by the tremors.

It lasted around 45 seconds, and was recorded as a 5.5 on the Richter scale. This is described as 'moderate: can cause major damage to poorly constructed buildings over small regions.' It releases the energy of a 178 kiloton bomb – but most of this is absorbed underground, relax. People still talk about the glasses tinkling and the ornaments rattling, as if a fleet of juggernauts was passing. Did the earth move for you?

Tectonic plates pushing together under the ocean can provoke a tsunami – that potentially lethal tidal wave that hits the coasts of the Indian and Pacific Oceans. Here in South Manchester, the problems presented by the Mersey bursting its banks, of course, don't compare.

But the problems still have to be solved. Since it rains a lot in the north-west (you've noticed?) and the Mersey is the only river in the area fed by the streams from the Peaks and the South Pennines, then yes, flooding of the riverside plain is going to be a constantly recurring cause of distress. The first overflow channel was created in 1799, but as the great number of nineteenth-century inundations were to show, it didn't really do the trick. In 1828, two Northenden lads, stranded by the sudden rise in water, had to climb into a tree until the deluge subsided the following morning.

Then, in July 1872, the flood reached as far as The Red Lion in Withington, where ducks took to paddling around the bar! A temporary lake up to 2 metres deep was formed below Didsbury Church, and the well-to-do houses and grounds of wealthy businessmen were turned into small islands along Wilmslow Road.

In the 1880s, floodwater tore away a bridge over Chorlton Brook. Building different levels into the riverbank helped, but the threat was reduced rather than eliminated.

The solution, which has been a blessing to many Didsbury and Northenden properties, was to construct a system of sluice gates at strategic points along the river. There's one near Jackson's Boat, and another south of Fletcher Moss. When the water level reaches a critical height the gates are opened, allowing the excess water to flow at right-angles to the river into specially constructed channels, whence it rejoins the Mersey way downstream. So far, it's worked a treat, and – unless any reader can correct me – any recent flooding has, fortunately, been relatively minor, and even quite photogenic.

LEVENSHULME'S 'PESTILENTIAL STREAMS'

In mid-Victorian times, before the absorption of Levenshulme village into the city of Manchester, the Fallowfield Brook supplied the locals' domestic water needs. This was despite the fact that upstream there was a bleachworks, and some of the residue from Reddish village found its way into the brook.

During the long, hot summer of 1885, as the smell from the stream grew fouler, some concern was expressed about the danger to health. Mr Estcourt, an expert in something or other, was summoned from Manchester. He had a look and a sniff, and incredibly pronounced the water safe: 'So long as lime from the bleachworks mixes with the brook it deodorises any malaria that might exist'. If there had been a froth on the surface, perhaps he would have recommended a nice cappuccino.

As the summer wore on, the debate over Levenshulme's 'pestilential streams' intensified. A heatwave brought about a garden hosepipe ban, with a fine of forty shillings for any transgressor. The hot weather, of course, was making matters worse. The brook near the Blue Bell Inn, despite giving off an 'abominable stench', didn't prevent hordes of children from playing in it. A Rusholme correspondent, calling himself 'AQUA', wrote to the local newspaper: 'How much good English beef has been spoiled through cattle drinking out of these running evils?'

There were outbreaks of disease, and it's noteworthy that Levenshulme's Medical Officer of Health, Mr Paton, resigned from the Local Board at the end of the summer. A second opinion from 'a leading medical gentleman' now asserted that the neighbourhood was in serious danger from the polluted water.

One of the problems was the jigsaw of responsibilities, since the water flowed through several areas. There were private landowners involved too: Mr Jannison of Belle Vue Gardens, for example. The necessary full co-operation between local boards and individuals proved difficult to achieve. The issue of contaminated water wasn't properly resolved until Levenshulme became part of Manchester, in 1909.

All of this makes it ironic that at the height of the 1885 heatwave, in neighbouring Rusholme, the smart new public baths were opened. They were on Monmouth Street, and owned by a Mr Royle. The water – 'invitingly pure' – was drawn from his own private well, and renewed every 24 hours. Entrance fees were sixpence during the day, or threepence after 6 p.m. A season ticket would have set you back a guinea – equivalent to a week's pay for a worker.

Rusholme, newly incorporated into Manchester, still retained some of its independent attitude: 'Mr Royle does not use the water of the great Corporation, which a deputation recently represented to the Moss Side local board as being neither fit for a bath nor for mixing with Scotch whisky.'

VICTORIA BATHS: EDWARDIAN WATER PALACE

When the Lord Mayor opened the Victoria Baths on High Street, Chorlton-on-Medlock, in September 1906, he baptised the sumptuous £59,000 Edwardian gem 'Manchester's Water Palace' – a title which has justifiably stuck.

Using cleaner and cheaper well water, the Palace offered a rare range of public facilities: three swimming pools, individual bathtubs, a laundry, club rooms, and fully equipped Turkish baths. Intended to serve the 80,000 population of the three surrounding boroughs of Longsight, Rusholme and St Luke's, its immediate huge popularity continued throughout most of the century.

For many years swimming was segregated, not only by gender, but also – a sign of the times – into first- and second-class male pools. So, depending on your social rank (or disposable income), you either had the privilege of the chandeliers, chute and diving boards for six old pence in first class, or you paid your three old pence and went and splashed with the plebs in the other, slightly smaller pool.

Gender segregation lasted until after the Second World War, when

The Edwardian Water Palace of Victoria Baths as it looks today. (Graham Phythian)

mixed bathing was permitted for two hours on Sunday mornings!

In its heyday, Victoria Baths was the crucible for future swimming stars. South Manchester Swimming Club had its base there, and several Olympians and Empire Games competitors, as well as celebrated Channel swimmer Ethel 'Sunny' Lowry (see page 62), used the pools for training.

And let's not forget the traumatic pleasures of the Turkish Baths, or Roman Baths, to give them their correct name.

I remember them well. You moved from room to room of increasing warmth, until the climax of trying to last the macho minute in the suffocatingly hot steam room, before bursting back out gasping for breath, skin scalding and innards simmering, into the merely tropical calidarium. There was also the climb down the ladder into the Aerotone, a cylinder of swirling warm water set into the floor: an earlier, more basic version of the jacuzzi.

Over the years, non-aquatic entertainments at the Baths have been diverse: the first-class pool could be covered over and used for bowling, dancing, or concerts. The Ted Heath Orchestra, Frankie Vaughan and Dickie Valentine performed there. The second-class pool has been known to double as a sports hall, with its peripheral balcony serving as a running track.

School swimming lesson in Victoria Baths, 1928. (Manchester
Central Library Local Images Collection: ref.m51828)

The building has been widely used in film and TV. Barry Gibb filmed his semi-autobiographical *Now Voyager* here, and TV crime buffs may be able to place scenes from *Prime Suspect*, *Life on Mars* and *Cracker*.

The bathing facilities were closed in 1993, but thanks to the BBC TV programme Restoration and a vigorous campaign by Friends of Victoria Baths (whose website is worth a look) the Grade II* listed building has been saved from demolition. The recently added star indicates that it is now considered a 'particularly important building of more than special interest'.

The address is now Hathersage Road, Rusholme, and there are guided tours every Wednesday afternoon from April to October.

The interiors still impress: the floor decorated with mosaics of starfish and jaunty dolphins, the ornate wall tiles and wrought-iron turnstiles and fitments, the pitch-pine balustrades and banisters, and the stained-glass windows with the sporting and 'angel of purity' themes.

In the meantime, we await the return of the water, and with it the Palace's full glories of yesteryear.

TEN

SOUTH MANCHESTER AT WAR

WITHINGTON AT WAR

Can you tell where the photograph on the opposite page was taken? Despite the flotilla of tents, possibly the nurses suggest the location, and perhaps that battleship of a building rings a bell. This was Withington Hospital, or, as it was known during the First World War when this picture was taken, Nell Lane Military Hospital. The building has been demolished, and the foreground is now the visitors' car park on Nell Lane. The tower of Didsbury's Christ Church (now on Princess Parkway) may be seen in the background.

The hospital was also used as a Prisoner of War camp, and one of the more famous guests of honour late on in the war was a U-Boat captain by the name of Karl Dönitz. He was to become Admiral Dönitz, supreme commander of the German fleet, in the Second World War, and – nominally and briefly – Hitler's successor in the last hours of the Third Reich.

The Second World War was a different beast: a war with 'no civilians', to quote Hitler. It was thought justifiable – by both sides – to advance the front line to domestic targets such as manufacturing, commercial and cultural centres. Civilian casualties, hitherto a regrettable by-product of the main business, were now fair game. It was in late 1940, after the enemy's first knock-back in the Battle of Britain, that Goering switched his point of attack, and the nation's cities became prime targets.

There is a well-known photo of the Scala cinema after the Luftwaffe had paid a visit on the night of 1 October. The road in front seems to have taken most of the blow, nonetheless the cinema was closed for three weeks

Nell Lane Military Hospital during the First World War.

for repairs. The film showing was Fifth Avenue Girl, starring Ginger Rogers. A house on Arnfield Road was bombed on the same night.

Withington Hospital was damaged, but remained in operation, not least as the place where the injured were taken and tended to. The Baths on Burton Road, suitably sandbagged and boarded up, were turned into a first aid post.

There was a lull in the air attacks, which then resumed with a vengeance over Christmas and New Year 1940/41. When people talk of the 'Manchester Blitz', this is usually the one they mean.

Nine people were killed on 1 January, even though they were in the supposed safety of an Anderson shelter, in the back garden of a house on Burton Road. After the all-clear was sounded, in the middle of the night, the wife of the minister of St Paul's Church on Wilmslow Road looked out into the garden. She made out a black shape which, she knew, wasn't part of the landscaping. She rang the Warden, who arrived with a UXB team. Fortunately, the bomb was rendered harmless, and was without further mishap.

There were defences: an anti-aircraft battery was stationed on Hough

End Fields, and a barrage balloon floated over Old Moat Park. And there was always the 12th (Withington) Reserve Battalion – our very own Dad's Army.

YANKS AND DAD'S ARMY

The following is based on a detailed and informative letter I received from Mrs J. Cowan, of Didsbury:

The Scala and Palatine cinemas were popular venues. The programmes were changed midweek, as was the newsreel, which would probably be a week or so old. After the Scala was damaged, and a landmine had landed in a tree in the vicarage garden, I was lucky to be given – and still have – a piece of the cord off the parachute.

The local Home Guard had their headquarters in Broadway, where I lived, in a house on the right, just past the first island. They met every Sunday morning to attend lectures on drill, etc.

Withington LDV (later the Home Guard) in 1940, with an appreciative audience.
(Manchester Central Library Local Images Collection: ref.m09638)

One Sunday morning they placed 'landmines' at the entrance to Broadway, plus a sentry, and everybody had to show their identity card (which we all had of course) when entering or leaving.

The Americans were billeted around here in 1944. I remember drawing back my bedroom curtains one morning to see all these American soldiers standing 'at ease' in two long rows along the grass in the centre of the road, together with all their kit, waiting to be taken to their 'new homes'. We had four billeted with us and they were all charming. They only slept in the house as they had their canteen nearby.

We learned later that they had arrived in Liverpool earlier that morning, having crossed over on the *Queen Mary*, then a troop ship.

In front of the Palatine cinema (where the DSS Offices are now) the Americans had erected their kitchen and canteen facilities, which were always busy,

One enduring memory I have is of seeing a company of soldiers marching in formation down Wilmslow Road towards Fog Lane/Lapwing Lane traffic lights. They were all shouting in unison, 'Hup – two – three – four', followed by some words in rhyme, then back to 'Hup ... etc.,' There were plenty of jeeps around, decorated with Betty Grable-type pin-ups and girls' names.

You mention a house in Arnfield Road which was bombed: a house in Parkville Road (adjacent to a cutting through to Henwood Road) also got a direct hit, and all the occupants, I believe, lost their lives. Houses in Moorland Road and Belfield Road were also hit. Where you see houses built to a different structure from those nearby, chances are that they were rebuilt after being bombed.

The boys had the ATC and the girls had the WJAC – the Women's Junior Air Corps. This met twice weekly: Friday evenings and Sunday mornings, at a school in Clyde Road.

The Manchester High School for Girls (part of their new school in Grangethorpe Road having been bombed) took over the Junior School at Manchester Grammar School, then situated in Central Road, West Didsbury, and also Broomfield School on Barlow Moor Road.

THE LUFTWAFFE PAY A VISIT TO CHORLTON

A photo taken from the *Manchester Evening News* of 2 May 1941 shows a young couple, looking remarkably unperturbed, standing in the ruins of their home, following a flying visit by the Luftwaffe the night before. It's a talismanic, morale-boosting image which quietly yet stirringly thumbs the nose at Hitler.

The couple – Mr and Mrs Mooney – had survived the blast because they had spent the duration of the air-raid in their indoor shelter, a solid steel construction designed and installed by a friend. It was no surprise that, after this incident, the shelter sold like hotcakes. The Mooneys were lucky: there were nine fatalities in the immediate area.

The couple were playing chess when they heard the whizzing of the falling missile. As the noise reached a crescendo, Mr Mooney's words to his wife were: 'Duck, this is ours.' Then the bomb hit, with 'the biggest smash I have ever heard.' Mrs Mooney's thoughts were: 'I never thought we would wake up in this world.'

For reasons of security, the precise geographical details aren't revealed in the report. 'The suburb of a

Mr and Mrs Mooney, looking remarkably unfazed in the ruins of their Chorlton home. (*Manchester Evening News*)

north-west inland town' is all we're given, but a bit of detective work can probably place the scene more accurately.

A map tracing from the National Archives gives a record of the attacks on Chorlton at 11.30 p.m. on 1 May 1941. The junction of Wilbraham Road and Corkland Road (then called Cavendish Road), the railway line (now the Metrolink line) and, further north, the public baths, are clearly shown. Four 250kg bombs were recorded as having fallen: the first two on the corner of Corkland Road and Chatfield Road; the second pair hit the railway embankment by Egerton Road. A giveaway for locating old bomb sites is the different housing architecture which replaced the uniform style of the demolished buildings. Sure enough, on the end of Chatfield Road, the houses are much more modern than the three-storey gabled and bay-windowed dwellings alongside and opposite.

There were few bombs dropped on the North West that night, as deteriorating weather conditions across the Channel prompted the early recall of the German planes. The *Manchester Evening News* headline told of a 'short, swift raid'. So it seems likely, unless any reader can prove differently, that what's left of the Mooneys' house was on the corner of Corkland Road and Chatfield Road.

On the home front, morale was a top priority. Despite the Luftwaffe raids, people were determined to keep leisure and cultural distractions up and running. In South Manchester in May 1941 there was a full cinema programme: the most popular films were Chaplin's *The Great Dictator*, Tommy Trinder in *Sailors Three*, and Bette Davis and Errol Flynn doing their bit in *The Private Lives of Elizabeth and Essex*. In town, Sir Malcolm Sargent was tenaciously conducting the Halle Orchestra. In the scaled-down North West Soccer League, Manchester United were playing Liverpool, and City had Blackpool as their opponents. Stanley Matthews, stationed with the RAF at Blackpool, would guest for local teams.

Across Europe, Nazi forces had had things mostly their own way, but 1941 saw the turning of the tide. The blitz had signally failed to sap the British resolve, a fact which is neatly and succinctly captured in the photograph.

WHEN A DOODLEBUG FELL ON DIDSBURY

Christmas Eve, 1944: the Second World War in Europe, everyone seemed to agree, was dragging towards an Allied victory, despite the stubborn German resistance since the D-Day landings. In England, the black-out regulations had ceased the previous September. Manchester had not suffered seriously from air-raids since the 'Christmas blitz' of 1940. Despite rationing and other wartime hardships, the general mood was one of cautious optimism and anticipation of the seasonal festivities.

Yet between 5 and 6 a.m. on 24 December, two whole squadrons of Luftwaffe bombers – a fleet of over fifty planes – had taken off from bases in Holland and were making their way under cover of darkness for the North of England. Moreover, their cargo wasn't the ordinary bomb quota. Carried beneath the starboard wing of each aeroplane was a V1: the terrifying 'doodlebug', Hitler's 'revenge weapon' flying bomb that had already wreaked havoc in London and the Home Counties.

The air-launched flying bomb attacks of that Christmas Eve claimed forty-two lives – mostly civilian – across the North. Thirty-one successful strikes were recorded: from Chester and Turton in the west to Hull in the east, and from County Durham in the north to Macclesfield Forest in the south. And one of the bombs fell on Didsbury.

It was around 5.30 a.m. Released from its parent Heinkel aircraft north of Stockport, the V1 began its descent over Cheadle, heading westwards directly for the densely populated residential area of Sharston, Wythenshawe. A local man, Mr R. Heywood, reported hearing the 'dull, pulsating roar' that 'seemed to shake the bed'.

Fortunately for Mr Heywood and the rest of the population of Sharston, when the V1's engine cut out the flying bomb took a turn to the right, heading north over Gatley. It then initiated a steep dive towards East Didsbury,

The deadly Doodlebug: Hitler's 'revenge weapon' that hit a field of Brussels sprouts in Didsbury.

crossing the River Mersey due south of what used to be Underbank Farm at the end of Millgate Lane, and where the Old Bedians rugby club headquarters are now. Fifty yards north of the river it hit the ground, detonating relatively harmlessly in a field of Brussels sprouts. The impact of the blast was nonetheless considerable: broken house windows were reported as far away as Fog Lane, Burnage, School Lane, Didsbury, and Altrincham Road, Northenden.

Nowadays there is no sign of the crater. There is an electricity pylon close to what was the bomb site. The immediate area now serves as playing fields.

Mercifully, when the bomb exploded in Didsbury in that early morning darkness, there were no casualties. Perhaps the only adverse effect – apart from the broken windows – was a slight restriction in the choice of vegetables for the locals' Christmas dinner.

ELEVEN

CUSTOMS AND CELEBRATIONS

RIDING THE STANG

One summer's evening in 1790, the village of Northenden bore witness to a bizarre procession. The heart of this boisterous cavalcade was a man dressed as a woman, seated back to front on a donkey. The beast was led by two other men, and all three were banging pots, kettles and pans.

The parade had made a tour of the village, collecting more participants on the way. By the time it reached its destination, the house of one Alice Evans, the crowd was huge and hilarious – making all manner of noise with metal objects, whistles, horns and trumpets.

Outside Evans' front door the racket stopped, and the man on the donkey recited:

Ran a dan, ran a dan, ran a dan.
Mrs Alice Evans has beat her
  good man.
It was neither with sword, spear,
  pistol or knife,
But with a pair of tongs she vowed
  to take his life.
If she'll be a good wife, and do so
  no more,
We will not ride stang from door
  to door.

Mrs Evans had been found guilty by mini-mob justice of walloping her poor husband with a pair of coal tongs. This custom of Riding the Stang was a sort of eighteenth-century unofficial ASBO, designed to make the wrong-doer mend his/her ways. Moreover, potential targets had their doorsteps swept as the procession made its way around the village.

Riding the Stang could be found in various guises up and down the British Isles as far back as

A boisterous cavalcade. (Detail from an eighteenth-century
watercolour, drawn by Rob Hall)

the Middle Ages. Stang is an old
Scandinavian word meaning ladder
or pole, and in some less civilised
versions of the tradition it was the
quarry who 'rode the stang', being
tied to a pole and generally roughed
up as he was paraded around the
village. This was the common practice in Sunderland, until matters
got out of hand round about the time
of the Northenden incident, and
an innkeeper suspected of helping

the pressgang wound up dead. The same happened to a wife-beater of Leith, who, after being tied to a tree branch and jolted around the village, was thrown into a nearby loch, where he drowned.

Other variations included the traditional New Year's Day shenanigans in Cumberland, Westmoreland and parts of Yorkshire. The first stranger encountered by the cacophonous band as it made its way around the village was straddled across a pole or bundled into a basket and carted off to the nearest pub, where they were expected to buy a drink. Small wonder that North Country folk preferred to stay at home on New Year's Day!

The original purpose of Riding the Stang, however, as in the medieval French custom of charivari and in our Northenden incident, was social censure and coercion through humiliation. The official process of the law of the land was totally ignored, and typical victims were adulterers, spouse-beaters, nags, barren couples, or even a man and wife whose ages were deemed to be incompatible. It was the prejudices of the village mind-set translated into action, and often the hullabaloo doubled as a simple pretext for disorder or the pursuit of a personal vendetta. Not a pleasant business, but a modern-day cynic would no doubt claim it had a higher success rate than ASBOs!

ALL THE FUN OF THE WAKES

Roll up! Roll up! Catch the greased pig and keep your family in bacon for a week. Pull a funny face through a horse's collar and win some ale. Eat an entire wax candle for a cash prize. Or if the thought of that turns your stomach, consume a treacle-loaf in one go. Win some money at the races: on foot, with wheelbarrow, or on a donkey. Try your luck at the prize stalls.

The patch of open land between what is now the Didsbury Inn (once the Ring o'Bells) and the Old Cock Inn was the scene of some decidedly original entertainment back in the nineteenth century.

Star turn must have been the gentleman with the dimensions of Peter Crouch, who drank a pint of buttermilk, then swallowed small, raw potatoes whole. Punters forked out a penny to put their ear against the man's stomach to hear the spuds going splosh into the liquid. No, I'm not making this up. It's in a book written by Alderman Fletcher Moss.

The festival began with the traditional rush-bearing procession on 5 August (St Oswald's Day), then from the following Sunday the village celebrated the annual Wakes holiday, when all shops and factories closed for a fortnight. Rush-bearing had an ancient purpose: that of spreading

Bringing home the bacon: chasing the greased pig. (Based on a
detail from an 1859 wood-engraving, drawn by Rob Hall)

rushes on church floors for insulation towards the end of summer. The tradition remained for many years in the form of a procession (first mentioned in Withington in 1603) and later accompanied by Morris Dancers and a band. The rushes on the cart were arranged into a tall edifice adorned with flowers, and from which there were hung various tankards and spoons, often of silver. The horses that drew the cart sported extravagant decorations on the top of their head. Fletcher Moss states that the rush cart which did the tour of the South Manchester

villages was made up at William Mee's Farm (later Hobson's Hall Farm) in Chorlton. This was on the site of the present cricket ground at the end of Ellesmere Road.

The early August celebrations in Didsbury in the late nineteenth century were in two distinct phases. The more respectable affair was the Horse and Horticultural Show, held in fields to the south of Stenner Lane.

Not everybody approved of the often rowdy Wakes, and the attendant shenanigans. Over in Rusholme, a local killjoy gave his opinion of the 1886 fairground:

This nuisance has made its bi-annual appearance, having cast anchor on the Croft, a vacant plot of land adjoining Princess St. The 'show' consists of the regulation merry-go-round, American swing-boats, shooting range, and a 'penny gaff' [a cheap or low-class place of entertainment]. The only attempt at originality is an instrument bristling with brass pipes. The sound given off puts a German military band in the shade.

With the arrival of the railways and cheap passenger travel, the Wakes underwent a fundamental change. Gradually home-grown activities were supplanted by a mass exodus to the seaside towns. Entertainment on tap took the place of the traditional recreations, but you can't help feeling something was lost. With the possible exception of the business with the greased pig, it sounds like fun.

ART TREASURES EXHIBITION 1857

For six months it was the art world's 'Greatest Show on Earth', and it transformed forever the international reputation of Manchester: the city that thrived on cotton and commerce would henceforth be seen as a cultural powerhouse too.

Occupying 17½ acres in the area now covered by the White City trading estate, the Exhibition was home to over 16,000 artefacts, and drew 1.3 million visitors over the summer of 1857. The range was as impressive as the quantity: from the old masters of Michelangelo, Rembrandt and Rubens, to modern photographic records of the Crimean War; from chronologically arranged suits of armour and military uniforms from famous battles, to ceramics, ivories and tapestries from across the world; from Hogarth drawings and contemporary watercolours to sculpture, ancient and modern.

The discovery and first showing of an unfinished Madonna and Child by Michelangelo, now on display at the National Gallery, caused a great deal of excitement, earning the picture the title of the 'Manchester Madonna'.

Having been granted royal patronage, the Exhibition was opened by Prince Albert on 5 May. A season ticket cost two guineas and daily entrance was an expensive 2s 6d, but this was reduced to a shilling on most days later in the month.

The cost was still prohibitive to many working-class Mancunians, but there were moves afoot to make the cornucopia of culture accessible to more sections of society. Letters to the *Manchester Courier* suggested a crèche at reception so that mothers who didn't have the services of a nurse could enjoy the exhibits fully, and there was a plea to the wealthy to allow their servants leave to go at 4 p.m. on a Monday. A request to reduce the entrance fee for the last few weeks was ignored, but paternalistic factory-owners organised and financed visits for large groups of their workers.

At the other end of the social scale, notable visitors included European royalty, Louis Napoleon, political movers and shakers Disraeli, Palmerston, and the Duke of Wellington, Florence Nightingale, and literary icons Charles Dickens, Elizabeth Gaskell, Nathaniel Hawthorne, and Poet Laureate Alfred Lord Tennyson. An anecdote doing the rounds about the Poet Laureate was that he was spotted leaving the no-smoking Exhibition area for a quiet drag in the adjacent Botanical Gardens.

As the punters strolled and marvelled, Charles Hallé conducted pieces by Mozart and Mendelssohn, as well as the specially-composed 'Exhibition Polka' – a daringly modern addition to the repertoire, and whose score became the pop hit of the year. These daily performances were the origins of the permanently established Hallé Orchestra.

Local businesses were quick to spot the commercial potential of

Art Treasures Exhibition – Main Hall. (Manchester Central Library Local Images Collection: ref.m58898)

attaching the 'Art Treasures' tagline to their advertisements. Must-have purchases that were plugged in the ads columns of the *Manchester Courier* included various refreshments, hire of bath chairs, musical scores, printed City guides, fans for ladies in the hot weather, special thin gloves in case you wanted to handle the exhibits, opera glasses, new ladies' fashions to be seen in, and flash ties and scarves for the men. The arrival of Queen Victoria at the end of July saw an increase in sales of fireworks, balloons, and commemorative medals. Manchester had not lost its celebrated business acumen!

The Exhibition was dismantled in October 1857, but the city would never be the same again. From now on it would be taken seriously as a cultural hub, with major and indelible contributions to the world of art, music, theatre and literature. This has made the pre-Exhibition foot-in-mouth of William Cavendish, the 7th Duke of Devonshire, grow in ironic comic quality over the years: 'What in the world do you want with art in Manchester? Why can't you stick to your cotton-spinning?'

You see, history can be fun.

CHRISTMAS 1860

South Manchester in 1860 had a white Christmas. The heavy snowfalls of a few days before had hardened with the frost, and under the clear blue skies the rural and village scenes must have glistened as fetchingly as on any Christmas card.

The exchanging of Yuletide cards existed at the time in certain circles, but the practice had yet to expand into a universal custom. Another twenty years, and it would be big business. However, the merry jingle of cash registers was already a familiar background to the celebrations. The *Manchester Courier* ran entire pages of adverts for festive wines and champagne, decorations, and suggestions for presents: tea caddies, inkstands, sewing machines, and sundry other household utilities. A quick trip up to Deansgate or Market Street was all it took, for those who could afford it. Less affluent families probably made their own presents: knitting, woodwork and other handicrafts would have done the necessary.

The Christmas shopper would have found toyshops there as well. What was the best-selling toy of 1860? Difficult to say, but well advertised, so presumably popular too, were dolls, rocking horses, cricket bats, and musical boxes (pricey, at £5 each).

Top indoor game aimed primarily at youngsters was 'Quartets', which seems to have been a forerunner of Trivial Pursuit. Each themed pack cost 1*s* 6*d*, and subjects included military engagements, geography, history, poets, and the Bible. The rules have disappeared with time, but the publishers enthused:

> These games, in a pleasing manner, impart information, strengthen the memory, and are invested with all the exciting interest of ordinary games of cards, without their injurious tendency.

The goose rather than the turkey would have been the centre piece of the Christmas Day meal, so South Manchester farms, as well as the market gardeners on Nell Lane, would have done a roaring seasonal trade. The alternative to goose was roast beef, and in poorer homes, rabbit. The custom of having a decorated fir tree ('that German toy', according to Dickens) had been launched by Queen Victoria and Prince Albert some years before. There were crackers containing sweets, but without the snap as they were unwrapped, and without the paper hats and mottoes or painful jokes inside.

Santa Claus was still a relatively obscure figure, a smattering of different European folk identities, clad in most colours other than red.

Some things haven't changed too much, as seasonal entertainment in 1860 included the pantomime. At the Theatre Royal, the pun-festooned script of *Cinderella* contained the usual topical references:

> Our railway's dangerous,
>   some old fogies say.
> The slow old coaches –
>   let them rail away.

St Andrew's Church, Ancoats, based on an 1833 print. (Phil Blinston)

On Christmas Day there was a concert at the Free Trade Hall: Handel's *Messiah* and Mendelssohn's *Elijah* were on the programme. More populist diversions were on offer over at Belle Vue, where the zoological gardens, museum, maze, and brass band would have cost the punter just 6*d* entrance fee. Free entertainment, weather permitting, could be had by sledging and skating on the Mersey Meadows. A piece of wood tied to the sole of the shoe served as an ice skate.

Christmas Eve 1860 was a memorable day for the parishioners of St Andrew's Church, Ancoats. The church clock had been in a state of disrepair for some time, so locals had organised a collection to pay for its cleaning and renovation. With a large crowd watching and applauding, Alderman Neild lit the gas which re-illuminated the ornate clock on the 1823 tower. The Christmas Day bells that rang out over Ancoats must have sounded all the sweeter!

PEOPLE'S PARK

Platt Fields Park, Fallowfield, celebrated its centenary in 2011. The full history may be found elsewhere, but visitors to the park's lush and landscaped 17 acres may wish to know if evidence of days gone by is still visible.

There's quite a lot there, for those willing to look. The oldest section of the park is the Anglo-Saxon earthwork Nico Ditch, now a protected Ancient Monument. (See page 104.)

Close to the ditch, on the way to Wilmslow Road, are the walled and sunken Shakespeare Gardens. They bear this name because Manchester merchant Mr Robinson, the owner of Ashfields, the manor house that used to dominate the immediate area, had the idea of cultivating here only plants, flowers and trees mentioned in the Bard's works. Shakespearean flora still in existence apparently number 178, so one wonders how many species were crammed into this small square of land. Nowadays there are tabs indicating spinach, beans, peas, turnips and sundry other vegetables, as the plots are being used for a Second World War 'dig for victory' hands-on historical experience.

A hundred yards or so closer to the road, half-hidden in the undergrowth, is the Cathedral Arch folly, another remnant of Ashfields. This portion of Manchester Cathedral was salvaged when the building underwent reconstruction in 1870. Ashfields house and stables were demolished in 1913, and the land added to the park.

The white seat near to the main road is dedicated to philanthropist William Royle. It was he who spearheaded a vigorous popular campaign to acquire the land for the people's use. The Platt estate came up for sale

The Cathedral Arch folly in Platt Fields. (Graham Phythian)

Platt Fields Park was officially opened on 7 May 1910, and was immediately and hugely popular, a status it hasn't lost over the years.

More recently it has also provided a focus for celebration of the multi-cultural character of neighbouring Rusholme. The centenary festivities included 1940s' wartime songs, reggae, Afro-pop, and a session from the Bollywood Brass Band. Memorable, as part of the Mega Mela festival in July 2011, was the world record Bollywood dance involving over 1,400 participants.

Platt Hall and grounds for sale. (Manchester Central Library Local Images Collection: ref.m58523)

twice: in 1901 and 1906. As may be seen from the photograph, the idea was to chop up the area for various purposes: mostly shops and housing.

In 1907, after long and ardent persuasion from Royle, the Manchester Corporation acquired the estate from the original part-buyer whose sacrilegious intention had been to raze Platt Hall and use the bricks to build shops.

So the 'people's park' or 'the lungs of the city' came into being. A small army of unemployed spent the best part of two years digging the hollows for the boating lake and outdoor swimming pool, and planting trees and shrubs.

This sketchy survey hasn't even mentioned Platt Hall Chapel, Grangethorpe, the First World War tank, the Second World War bombs, the air-raid shelters, the model railway, the bandstand, the statue of Abraham Lincoln, Speakers' Corner, the DIY pizza oven …

In mitigation, to fill in the gaps I heartily recommend the Platt Fields History Walks. They take place throughout the summer, starting from the lakeside buildings. Full details are in the local press, or the website: www.plattfields.org

JOLLY GOOD COMPANY

Panto time's but once a year, and as far as amateur dramatics are concerned, here in South Manchester we're spoilt for choice. Notable for their trademark mix of song, dance and off-the-wall humour are amateur dramatic group Chorlton Players.

Chorlton Players have an interesting history. They were once called

The old St Werburgh's Parish Community Hall, demolished in 1963.
(Manchester Central Library Local Images Collection: ref.m18342)

St Werburgh's Amateur Dramatic Society (or SWADS to the cognoscenti) and their origins lie embedded in church traditions. Next door to the church, where the Community Hall is now, there was once a wooden hut, big enough to squeeze in a fair-sized audience for modest shows. Way back in 1957, for example, Chorlton's Young Conservatives put on *Little Red Riding Hood* (I think I've got the colour right). At around the same time, the church Junior Group started to stage Passion Plays at Easter, and 'entertainments' at Christmas. There was a Social Group too: one of their notable coups was to persuade Herman's Hermits to perform at the Hall. Since Juniors have a tendency to grow older over the years, it was a natural progression for the ex-Juniors and the Social Group to combine, with a view to staging plays.

The new Hall was built in 1963, and it seems that the separate Drama Group was formed that year. The following February the Parish Magazine recorded the staging of *Little Lambs Eat Ivy*, 'a light comedy in three acts', and then the farce *Rookery Nook* in May. At the first ever AGM in June, five secular plays were pledged for the following season, starting with the melodrama *Shadow in the Sun*. It's noteworthy that for each play there were three performances: Friday, Saturday, and the following Monday. In making Sunday the central day

of the run, the idea seems to have been to emphasise the role of the Church. Perhaps the sermon included a plug. The immensely popular *Goodnight Mrs Puffin* – a humorous drama about 'the charwoman from Clapham Junction who has dangerous dreams which come true' – was staged the following January (1965). This was followed by Terence Rattigan's *Separate Tables*, and then the comedy thriller *The Gazebo*.

It was in October 1965 that SWADS made it into the big time, with their first review in the *Manchester Evening News*. The play was the J.B. Priestley standard *When We Are Married*. The critic spoke of a 'thoroughly polished show', which was 'well up to the standard of this first-class company'. Director Geoffrey Kellett delivered the goods again just over a month later, also starring in the thriller *The Two Mrs Carrolls*. The whole cast was mentioned in dispatches: Shirley Southern ('a very fine performance indeed'), Linda Smith, Jean Davies, Isobelle Cooper, Shirley Male, John Hiddleston, and Michael Armitage. Where are they now? If you recognise your name on this list, please get in touch!

SWADS became Chorlton Players some ten years ago. The productions are more ambitious than in the early days, but the tradition of high quality theatre remains unbroken.

MARATHON MEMORIES

South Manchester has long had an affinity with the Marathon, the 26-mile and 385-yard footrace that has fired the imagination for well over a century. The old Fallowfield football and cycling ground was often the hub of the event: the 1909 Manchester Marathon finished there, and the stadium was also the start and finish of the races held in the city between 1921 and 1936.

The first great popular Marathon explosion of the early 1980s, in which the world and his wife became convinced they could have a go, was harnessed in 1982 by Piccadilly Radio. That year it attracted over 8,000 runners. The course started and finished in Platt Fields, and its route took in a sizeable chunk of west and south Manchester.

The race actually began on the main Wilmslow Road just outside Platt Fields. For the vast majority of runners, there was a preliminary period of dawdling and shuffling forward, whilst somewhere up ahead the elite competitors were racing away, until the log-jam finally cleared, and the ordinary mortals could start running. The course then took you up Oxford Road, under the Mancunian Way (the communal, OGGI! OGGI! OGGI! chant resounding over the clatter of footsteps); over Deansgate and past the Granada studios, then onto the endless Liverpool Street. The stretch along the East Lancashire Road took you past the golf course, useful for those wishing to nip into the bushes to spend a penny. The Worsley roundabout marked ten miles, a nice landmark, as here you 'turned the corner' and were heading back towards Manchester.

There were drinks stations every three miles, which gave you something to look forward to in those increasingly painful miles. The long road into Stretford was next, over Barton Bridge, and aiming for that huge red 'K' on the Kellogg's factory at Trafford Park. Then through Moss Side, with the jazz band lifting the spirits! Three more long stretches to go (Princess Road, Barlow Moor Road, Kingsway) and you were nearly there: Birchfields Road, Dickenson Road, and at last the blessed trees and crowds of Platt Fields once more. You'd made it!

Runners cross Barton Bridge during the 1983 Piccadilly Marathon. (Trafford Archives)

Winner in 1982 was local fireman Kevin Best. The course soon gained a reputation for being fast, as there were no major hills. The 1983 race was started by Olympic runner Ron Hill, firing the gun from the cradle of a crane high above Wilmslow Road. He was then lowered down to ground level so he could join the race! Champion Lady in both years was London's Leslie Watson, who considered the Platt Fields finish to be the 'best in the world outside New York'.

Star competitor in 1984 was world record holder Ian Thompson, and star prize was a Ford Escort XR-3. Thompson held off spirited challenges and won the car.

By 1985 the Marathon boom was beginning to fade, and Piccadilly Radio organised their last Manchester Marathon. Its legacy, besides the millions of pounds raised by the runners for charity, was a template on how to put on such a massive event with efficiency and razzamatazz.

TWELVE

EARTH, WOOD, BRICK AND STONE

A DITCH IN TIME

Ryebank Fields is that shaggy open space on Chorlton's western edge, next door to the verdant expanse of Longford Park. Every now and again the fate of the Fields comes up for discussion: last time around, some developers wanted to build some houses there.

One of the arguments for leaving the Fields be – or at least treating them with kid gloves – is that they are crossed east to west by a shallow and overgrown but visible ditch.

This isn't conservation gone batty. There's every likelihood that we're talking about Nico Ditch, a thousand-year-old Anglo-Saxon earthwork. Its extension three miles due east in Platt Fields is a Scheduled – and therefore protected – Ancient Monument, complete with heritage stone bearing a potted history.

The earthwork's original 6-mile-long course was south-west from Ashton Moss, across the area now covered by the Audenshaw reservoirs and the M60. Beyond that it is a feature of Denton Golf Course. You can trace its line across the links for some 250 yards, and there is one well preserved stretch which gives its name to the 12th hole. According to Club Secretary and local historian Ian McIlvanney: 'A golfer with a good tee shot down the fairway on the twelfth will never realise the Ditch is there. Slice your shot and you will get to know Nico Ditch very well!'

The line of the earthwork then crossed modern-day Hyde Road and curved to the west through Gorton, parallel to what is now Laburnum Road. There are short stretches still visible in Gorton Cemetery and by Wayland Road South in Ryder Brow – and old maps bear this out.

It then struck due west, along the southern edge of Melland playing

The Ditch on Denton Golf Course. (Graham Phythian)

fields bordering Levenshulme (where it may be clearly seen alongside the path), then followed the line of the present day Matthews Lane and Old Hall Lane as far as Platt Fields.

West of Platt Fields, conjecture starts to creep in. A short section of an old earthwork used to be in evidence near to Chorlton baths, between Buckingham Road and Manchester Road, but the area has now been built on. Similar in appearance to, and directly aligned with, the sections further east, this was quite possibly a small segment of Nico Ditch. On Ryebank Fields, the ditch peters out

as it reaches the hedgerow marking the perimeter of Longford Park. Local resident David Barrow can recall the ditch being 'at least a metre deep, before they built the football pitches in the sixties'.

Why was the earthwork built? It's tempting to think in terms of a defensive structure, *à la* Offa's Dyke, especially since the Danes were throwing their weight around in the area at the time it is supposed to have been constructed. There was also a bank on the northern side of some sections, which seems to support the military argument.

The Nico Ditch heritage stone in Platt Fields. (Graham Phythian)

THE SIEGE OF WYTHENSHAWE HALL

However, recent research and archaeological digs have determined that the mound was a much later addition. Besides, defensive ditches were usually constructed to a V-shape, whilst the shallow U-shape of Nico Ditch seems to suggest a boundary line.

Why 'Nico'? The most plausible reason is that the word is a corruption of the Anglo-Saxon *micel*, meaning great or big. The earthwork is first mentioned in a legal document of around AD 1200, in which 'Mykelldiche' is referred to as a land boundary in Audenshaw.

Wythenshawe Hall, the central portion of which with its huddle of half-timbered structures, has survived from Tudor times, today sits agreeably amidst its well-tended gardens, offering museum tours and a tea room. It's hard to believe that this quiescent old duffer, a Grade II listed building, stubbornly resisted

A modern view of the Tudor section of Wythenshawe Hall. (Graham Phythian)

a three-month siege by Cromwell's troops during the Civil War.

The Hall was a garrison for Royalist troops, and of strategic importance since it was close to the ford over the Mersey at Northenden. The Parliament forces had taken the ford, but in order to secure it they had to make sure that the Wythenshawe Hall garrison was scotched.

The siege began in November 1643, during one of those wickedly cold winters that were common in seventeenth-century England. Robert Tatton was in charge of the Royalist troops (some eighty men) and with possible reinforcements engaged elsewhere in Cheshire, this isolated pocket of resistance was not expected to hold out for long.

But the siege dragged on throughout the winter. Parliamentarian Captain Adams was relying on support from Manchester, but the snow-clogged roads prevented the delivery of heavy cannon. Moreover, his troops were inexperienced in the disciplined approach necessary for successful siege warfare. Camping in the snow, or billeting in the hamlets of Lawton Moor and Northern Moor, was likely to have undermined morale. The Northenden recruits must have felt a great temptation to nip off home for a hot toddy!

The Royalists made the most of their sheltered position, and would make the occasional surprise attack on the enemy, using the Hall banqueting house as an outpost. The larder was well stocked, at least at the beginning of the siege: there was salted beef, cheese, oats, corn, wheat, peas and beans, and enough beer to allow a soldier a pint a day. (You can do the maths.) Wheat flour would have been eked out with rye, to make substandard, but edible, maslin bread. There was also a swine park adjoining the Hall, so there was bacon while stocks lasted.

It was on 27 February 1644 that Cromwell's troops finally won the day. The snows had melted, so the cannon had arrived from Manchester. With enough supplies left for just one more week, the garrison surrendered, and Robert Tatton escaped to Chester.

The romantics believe that on the final day of the siege a serving girl by the name of Mary Webb took revenge for her fiancé's death in the struggle by taking a pot shot with a rifle at Captain Adams, the Parliamentarian commander, as he sat on a wall outside the Hall. The detail is unsupported, but Adams was indeed shot dead on the last day of the siege, by a person unknown. They say that Mary Webb's ghost still haunts Wythenshawe Hall.

The Hall is open to visitors on Saturdays throughout the summer.

THE CHEQUERED HISTORY OF HOUGH END HALL

Like a much-missed old friend who arrived late to the party, Hough End Hall at last re-opened for business in February 2010. As reported in the local press, the venerable building's latest identity was that of a bar and restaurant.

The Hall was built in 1596: the year which saw the death of Sir Francis Drake, Shakespeare's *Romeo and Juliet*, and the installation of the first flush toilet at the royal residence of Richmond Palace. The original owner of Hough End Hall was a Sir Nicholas Moseley, given his title by Queen Elizabeth I for ploughing a substantial portion of his drapery profits into supplying soldiers and ships to fight Ireland and Spain. Upon being knighted and assuming the office of Lord of the Manor of Manchester, he changed the spelling of his name to Mosley, and awarded himself a coat of arms which bore the Latin motto *MOS LEGEM REGIT* – 'custom rules the law' – the sort of bilingual pun that had the Elizabethan upper crust rolling in the aisles.

The house has had a chequered history, reflecting the character, trade and fortunes of those living in it. The earliest pictures show an attractive, three-storey, ivy-clad brick mansion surrounded by a low wall and decorative trees. Sir Nicholas lived there on his move from London until his death in 1612. His grandson Edward, cavalier in both senses of the word, frittered away most of the family fortune in supporting the Royalist cause in the Civil War. He was forced to sell the house and surrounding estates to Sir Edward Mosley of the Hulme branch of the family.

Sir Edward's daughter Anne married Sir John Bland in Chorlton Chapel in 1685, so Hough End Hall and the grounds passed to the Bland family. Unfortunately after three dissolute generations of wassailing and wenching, the financially embarrassed Blands were forced to sell the house on to the Egertons of Tatton (1756). Samuel Egerton let it out as a farm, so its identity and clean architectural lines were blurred by a jumble of barns and outbuildings. The Egertons cannibalised the oak fittings and fine staircase to help embellish Tatton Hall. The reduced, partially disfigured building has also seen service as a toolhouse, smithy, and more recently, with some modern renovations, a private house and offices.

Hough End Hall was once close to being demolished, but happily was deemed worthy of preservation as a Grade II listed building. This is defined by the City Council as a

An old drawing of Hough End Hall, probably when owned by the Egerton family. (Manchester Central Library Local Image Collection: ref.m47822)

'particularly significant building of more than local interest'.

Reinvented as a short-lived fun bar and restaurant in the 1980s, and since then available only for the occasional private function, it has lain unused for too long. Nestling between Mauldeth Road West and Chorlton High School, and cowering below the massive office block, it can easily be overlooked by passers-by. However, as of February 2010 the old friend was back, dispensing hospitality and good cheer!

At the time of writing (2012) the Hall once more awaits a new owner.

THE GHOSTS OF JACKSON'S BOAT

Ghosts have had a bad rap recently. I blame TV: such series as *Most Haunted*, despite all the urgent whispering, eerie music and atmospheric lighting, each time turned out to be as spooky as *Fifi and the Flowertots*.

Purists may want to seek out the real thing. The Jackson's Boat pub certainly looks the part on a dark night: isolated amidst fields and woodland, the river flowing silently below, with its craggy old brick exterior and timbered decor, in the 1980s it was short-listed by Teacher's Whiskey in the search for the 'most authentic haunted pub' in Britain.

It has an interesting past. The original building dates from 1663: a different age, when Samuel Pepys was writing his diary, and New York was still called New Amsterdam. In the 1730s, the old wooden building was a meeting place for local Jacobites who, with the help of a bowl of punch, discreetly drank the health of the Stuart Pretender. The nearby ferry, run by a farmer by the name of Jackson, gave the inn its name. The present hostelry was built around 1800, and the toll bridge, giving the pub its temporary title of The Bridge Inn, followed in 1816. The original bridge was swept away in a flood, and the present one dates from 1881. The pub has been the venue for illegal cock fights, and, during floods, it was not unknown for ale to be served to boats from an upstairs window!

So what's all this about things that go bump in the snug?

There's a famous photo of Jackson's Boat from 1901, in which there appear to be two semi-transparent figures: a diminutive monk on the path, and a vaguely human shape on the bridge.

In the book *Haunted Pubs of Britain and Ireland* (1984), landlord Tom Gray speaks about resident ghost George the Jacobite in his Highland kilt, quietly supping his virtual noggin at the bar. He says his barmaids knew and tolerated the spectral sitting tenant.

More recently there have been tales of hammering on the front door at dead of night, with the porch area

Most haunted? The famous photograph supposedly showing the spectral
monk on the path, and the ghostly figure on Jackson's Bridge.

deserted. Current landlord David Hall, alone in the pub one morning, heard a child's giggle. He tells of normally placid dogs growling and barking at apparent fresh air in one particular corner. Electrical fittings have behaved freakishly. Ghost writer Adele Kain tells of a dark shadow frequently seen moving through the bar area, and disembodied voices calling the staff by name. A mysterious dawn staccato sound, however, turned out to be blackbirds' beaks tapping against a downstairs window!

Paraquest, Trafford's own ghostbusters, sent a camera team down the cellar, but apart from an allegedly aggressive bucket, little of interest appeared to happen. (The video is on the internet.)

Believers will speak of a hub of psychic energy, of unhappy elements of the past reaching out to try and influence the present, where they have no right to be. Cynics may wonder what brands of spirits have been generating the stories.

Perhaps it's just coincidence that one of Britain's ancient ley lines passes plumb through three nearby places with supposedly supernatural connections: Alderley Edge, Wythenshawe Hall, and Jackson's Boat. There's surely a rational explanation for all this ghostly palaver – isn't there?

A TUNNEL VISION

What's the connection between Mount Snowdon, the Channel Tunnel, and a gravestone in a Northenden churchyard?

The answer is a gentleman by the name of Sir Edward Watkin, one of those multi-tasking Victorian technocrats who used his wealth and influence to become involved in a wide range of public endeavours.

On Snowdon the Watkin path bears his name. That's the route up the mountain from the A498 near the Nant Gwynant car park, easy-peasy scenic until it hits the formidable rocky slope south-east of the summit, when suddenly

Sir Edward Watkin.

you're climbing Mount Doom. Along the way you can see the ruins of Watkin's summer retreat, The Chalet, and the Gladstone Rock, which bears a plaque commemorating the 1892 opening of the path.

Ever the railways entrepreneur, Watkin was responsible for the Athens-Piraeus line, as well as being instrumental in the development of the Indian and Canadian railway systems. However, the project which dominated the last forty years of his life was the Channel Tunnel.

First mooted in Napoleonic times as a stagecoach route, an underground railway line linking England to France caught Watkin's imagination in the 1860s, while he was Liberal MP for Stockport. Although the first sod would not be cut for another twenty years, the supporters of the project were to fight tooth and nail with the objectors for the rest of the century.

Watkin spotted the commercial potential of such a scheme, besides the obvious advantages of convenience and comfort. A journey time of thirty minutes was estimated, as against the hour and a half of gut-churning purgatory that frequently marred a ferry crossing.

The Stock Exchange launch of the Submarine Continental Railway Company raised a heartening £250,000. Eventually, in 1881, the scheme received Parliamentary blessing, and the English side of operations began west of Dover, below the Shakespeare Cliffs. In the early months progress was rapid, reaching a rate of 60 metres a week. At about the same time, the French began boring through the chalk at Sangatte, a few kilometres down the coast from Calais.

Watkin knew how to sell the idea. Champagne receptions were held in the tunnel, and guests included the Prince of Wales, the Archbishop of Canterbury, and the Lord Mayor of London. All enthused, as did a delegation from the French end, including Ferdinand de Lesseps of Suez Canal fame. Even the initially sceptical Gladstone was won round.

Unfortunately, the War Office, who had some powerful and influential players on their side, was expressing displeasure. Would not the tunnel facilitate invasion from a European state?

Bugbear of the time was the newly unified and militarist Germany, and the popular fear was skilfully played on by the War Office. In vain did Watkin and his supporters point out that an army emerging from the narrow egress would be sitting ducks for two or three well placed machine gunners. Besides, flooding or blocking the tunnel at short notice would be an easy matter.

All this fell on deaf ears, and a Parliamentary ruling, followed by a High Court order, stopped the drilling in spring 1882. Catching the mood of negativity, the French called a halt to proceedings at the Sangatte end.

Each team had created a passage of around 2 kilometres, but that was to be the limit for over a century.

Watkin continued to campaign, but to no avail. He retired from active public life and returned to the family home at Rose Hill Cottage, Northenden (the future orphanage and remand home). Though by now old and infirm, he never lost his belief in the viability of the tunnel, continually pestering Parliament with Bill after Bill. His persistence led to the rather mean pun in his obituary in *Vanity Fair* in April 1901: 'the bore of the Channel Tunnel'. Sir Edward's gravestone may be seen at St Wilfrid's Church, Northenden.

When work on the Channel Tunnel recommenced in 1986, the original 1880s' workings were discovered, still in excellent condition.

IT HAPPENED AT 'THE TOWERS'

Picture the scene. It's a June day in 1882, and a steady stream of horse-drawn carriages and cabs are trotting down Wilmslow Road in Didsbury, making their way to the entrance lodge by the cricket club. From here the carriages take the long driveway through the parkland to the château-style mansion of 'The Towers', home of industrialist Daniel Adamson.

Channel Tunnel workings, 1882. (*London Illustrated News*)

At the ornate front doorway the top-hatted passengers leave their vehicle and mount the steps. There is an aura of wealth and power about them, and as they enter the great house, the owner greets them: mayors, aldermen, mill owners, engineers and financiers, over seventy of the rich and influential elite of the north-west. They have come from as far afield as Oldham, Macclesfield, Warrington, and the Lancashire cotton towns.

The purpose of this high-powered meeting, in that age of bold technology and ambitious, confident ideas, was to propose the financing of The Manchester Ship Canal. Exorbitant taxes on the Port of Liverpool's imports – nearly half of which were destined for Manchester – were crippling the cottonopolis. The canal would be a means of by-passing Liverpool, and bringing goods directly to Manchester.

The scheme had its detractors, not least those whose income would be curtailed. For obvious reasons, the city of Liverpool and the railway companies were the most outspoken critics.

Adamson, however, had done his homework. He referred to the engineering achievement and financial success of the Suez Canal, and closer to home, the work recently done to streamline the Clyde and the Tyne. The scheme would also be very lucrative: a revenue of some £750,000 per annum was predicted.

The Towers, Didsbury, now part of a business park. (Graham Phythian)

The resolution to form 'The Manchester Tidal Navigation Company' was made, and the proposal to build the canal was put before Parliament. After three years of tough opposition, in August 1885 an Act of Parliament was passed allowing the Ship Canal to be built. The grounds of The Towers were the scene of a celebration party, at which a brass band played and ten barrels of beer were consumed.

It's not beyond the bounds of possibility that the sumptuous architecture of The Towers had a part to play in that decision of June 1882. The subliminal message to the future shareholders was that anyone who owned a mansion as grand as this wasn't going to put them wrong.

The Towers had been completed in 1872 on the south-eastern edge of Didsbury village, on a hill overlooking the Mersey valley. Its architect was Thomas Worthington, who also designed the Albert Memorial, and what was to become Withington Hospital.

The red brick and yellow sandstone building calls to mind the château at Blois, but with some Gothic touches. For example, there was a competition amongst the stonemasons to see who could design the most hideous gargoyle. Some grotesque inventions saw the light of

Close up of the gargoyles. (Graham Phythian)

day: the deformed animals and birds gurning and straining above the side and rear windows are creatures from a bad dream by Hieronymus Bosch. Toasted cheese suppers must have really packed a punch in those days.

It was originally built to house *Guardian* editor John Edward Taylor Junior, but it's debatable whether he ever actually spent much time there. The story goes that his wife took one look at the building and declared it wasn't for her, as she preferred Kensington.

A couple of years later Daniel Adamson bought the house, and, according to the 1881 census, was living there with his wife Mary and eight domestic servants.

One of Adamson's many interests was brass bands, and when the Astley Victoria Band from his native Dukinfield was in need of a sponsor, he readily stumped up the cash to enable them to continue. In gratitude, they renamed themselves the Adamson Reed Band (now the Adamson Military Band). In August 1889, having travelled in from Dukinfield by wagonette, they gave a concert at The Towers.

Adamson the visionary and philanthropist died in 1890, sadly several years before the opening of the canal. His grave and monument may be seen in Southern Cemetery.

During the First World War, The Towers was used as a recreational retreat for wounded soldiers, and then in 1920 the British Cotton Industry Research Association bought the place: a snip at £10,000. A major contributor to this purchase was cotton baron and Stockport

Didsbury celebrates the success of Adamson's Ship Canal venture in 1884.
(Manchester Central Library Local Image Collection: ref.m54885)

Tory MP William Greenwood, who asked for the building to be named after his daughter Shirley. This was agreed, which is why the building and estate became known as The Shirley Institute.

The Second World War saw the development at the institute of vital fabrics which contributed significantly to the war effort: khaki webbing, a de-lousing belt, and rot-proof material for use in combat in the humid Far East. A couple of inventions have peacetime descendants: the flea-resistant cat collar was first produced here, as was the wind- and waterproof material Ventile. Nowadays, if you can hear a birdwatcher as he shuffles around, he's probably wearing Gore-Tex. If he's silent, chances are his gear is made of Ventile.

Over the years, The Towers technology park/business estate has shown an impressive affinity for royalty. New buildings have been opened by the Duke of York (later King George VI), the Duchess of Kent, HRH Princess Margaret, and HRH Princess Anne.

The Towers now stands on the private ground of a business park, housing several small companies with science or technology connections. Manchester Heritage organises the occasional public tour.

THIRTEEN

ICONS AND ECHOES

ROMAN COINS FOUND IN RUSHOLME

One day in October 1896, a young lad, hoping to earn a few extra pence, went foraging for lost golf balls on the Anson Club course. This was roughly in the area which is now occupied by the housing estate in the square formed by Dickenson Road, Slade Lane, Old Hall Lane, and Birchfields Road.

Reasoning that the Gore Brook – which then wound its way across the links – would have a magnetic attraction for wayward balls, the lad started poking around the stream's muddy banks. Where the famously malodorous brook reached the tree-lined Birchfields Road – beyond which lay the new and prettily landscaped Park – the seeker unearthed something which probably made him forget all about golf balls. He pulled from the mud a wooden box which contained around 200 ancient Roman bronze and copper coins.

It is not recorded whether the youngster was rewarded for his find, but within days the cache was appropriated by Owens College Museum, which was later to move up Wilmslow Road and become Manchester Museum. Mr W.S. Churchill (no, not that one, he was in Bombay at the time) gave a talk on the coins at the next meeting of the Lancashire and Cheshire Antiquarian Society.

Although the intrinsic value of the coins was low – Mr Churchill stated it was the 'hoard of a man in humble circumstances' – the collection was of great interest to the historian. The coins generally were in poor condition, but enough details were legible for them to be dated with some accuracy. The Emperor Gallienus and his family figured on around a dozen of them, but more plentiful, and of better quality, were the coins bearing the head of the so-called usurper Emperors: Postumus and Tetricus.

In the middle of the third century the Roman Empire was in a state of near-collapse. Barbarian tribes were running the frontier legions ragged, and at one time inflation was at a galloping one thousand per cent. A significant splinter Empire was formed from Gaul, part of Spain, and most of Britain. The rival Emperors, usually generals popular with their troops, created their own government and coinage. This wasn't idle posturing: it was during the Pretenders' generally successful rule that the wooden Manchester fort at Castlefield was rebuilt in stone, and the port at Lancaster was refortified to repel invaders.

So the cache of coins may be dated at around 270 AD, or the final year of the reign of the Emperor Claudius II, whose head appears on eleven of the coins.

Why were they hidden? Historians say that a number of such coin hoards have been found across the Roman Empire, especially dating from the lawless years of the mid third century. Perhaps the owner feared invasion, or robbery as he travelled the wild and uninhabited spaces of Roman Britain.

The hiding place was in open country-side, but at a point two miles south-east of the Mamucium fort, and half a mile west of the Roman Road (now the A6 Stockport Road – see page 46) on the obvious landmark of the brook. So whoever hid the coins must have been pretty certain of relocating the hoard at a later date. Perhaps death or some other calamity prevented his return.

It's not too fanciful to claim that virtually every street or field in South Manchester hides a slice of history. Or in this case, two slices, one on top of the other.

FAREWELL TO THE FAMOUS

Postumus, the usurper Emperor.

Here's one you can try down the pub: what have all the following got in common?

Sir Matt Busby, CBE, KCSG (1909-1994). After playing for Manchester City and Liverpool before the Second World War, Sir Matt also picked up a Scotland cap before turning his post-war attentions to football management. His achievement was to build three great teams, surviving the Munich air disaster to attain the crowning glory of the European Cup in 1968.

L.S. Lowry (1887-1976). Although associated with Salford, Laurence Stephen Lowry was actually born in Stretford. His supposedly 'naïve' portraits and industrial scenes still have a magnetic capacity to linger in the mind. Once seen, a Lowry isn't easily forgotten. The artist holds the record for the most number of honours declined: OBE (twice), CBE, Companion of Honour, and a Knighthood.

Sir John Alcock, KBE, DSC (1892-1919). Born on Seymour Grove, the aviator is one half of the famous Alcock and Brown, who were the first to fly the Atlantic. The 16-hour and 12-minute flight netted for Alcock his share of the £10,000 *Daily Mail* prize, as well as a knighthood from King George V. His tragic death in an air crash in fog near to Rouen six months later was mourned by millions.

Wilfred Pickles, OBE (1904-1978). Born in Halifax, Pickles built up a northern cult following due to his uncompromising radio persona: 'And to all in the north, good neet [sic].' He was a familiar comedy figure on early British TV (catchphrase: 'What's on the table, Mabel?'), and was memorable playing Billy Liar's father in the Schlesinger film.

Billy Meredith (1874-1958). Born in Chirk, North Wales, Meredith became arguably the greatest footballer of his generation. He was certainly the most durable: his football career began aged 18 playing for Chirk. Greater glories ensued with Football League teams Northwich Victoria, Manchester City, then United, then City again. (See page 43.) His last League game was played at age 49. He played for Wales forty-eight times, scoring eleven goals.

Daniel Adamson (1820-1890). Featured elsewhere in this book (see pages 113-117), he was the Didsbury industrialist who launched the idea of the Manchester Ship Canal. Also a much admired philanthropist and social visionary, his original intention was for the canal's workers to share in the profits.

Sir Robert McDougall (1871-1938). As in McDougall's flour. Sir Robert's wide-ranging generosity, from restoring buildings and donating them to the National Trust, to financing essay prizes and new projects, could easily be the subject of a series of articles.

Maria Jasnorzewska (1891-1945). Celebrated Polish poetess and playwright, she left her native country in 1939 to live in Manchester. Her poems have a sensual, lyrical quality, and her feisty, politically aware plays have been compared to Molière and Oscar Wilde.

Sir Alfred Ernest Marples, PC (1907-1978). He was the Transport Minister whose legacies to the nation were yellow lines, seat belts, and parking meters.

Tony Wilson (1950-2007). Wilson helped blow away the cobwebs from the Manchester popular music scene in the 1990s. The Haçienda nightclub, Factory Records, Happy Mondays and Joy Division all owed their prominence to his influence.

As the reader has possibly already guessed, the common link is that all the above have graves in Southern Cemetery, off Barlow Moor Road.

KNOW YOUR WOOD

If you've not already done so, take the time to visit the Levenshulme

Former Levenshulme Town Hall – now the Craft Village. (Graham Phythian)

Antiques and Crafts Village, which celebrated its thirtieth birthday in 2011. It's in an unmissable red brick building that used to be the Town Hall, situated on Stockport Road a half-mile or so south of the railway station.

The interior is a warren of shops, galleries, craft studios and antiques by the roomful. The credentials are impressive: the next time you watch a *Harry Potter* film, check out the furniture in Dumbledore's study. Many of the artefacts started life here, at Lee Wright's workshop in the yard out the back. Lee has also supplied furniture for the *Coronation Street* set, as well as an ornate chair for a Saudi prince.

Upstairs the genial Ken gave me a crash course on how to be – or at least sound like – an *Antiques Road Show* expert. Basically you have to 'know your wood'. There is a ranking order to the value of material used to create antique furniture: from plebeian pine, up through oak, mahogany and rosewood, to ultra-posh ebony and other exotic woods. Also, the more elaborate the design, and therefore the more wood lost in the construction, the more money you should expect to pay for the item.

Ken recently sold up, and his studio space is now occupied by Ronnie, who plays a Spartan in re-enactments of Ancient Greek battles. His sword and shield looked fearsomely persuasive, but on closer inspection turned out to be a relatively harmless construct of fibre-rod, foam and latex. Nonetheless, sword fight training is

Ronnie the Spartan. (Graham Phythian)

held in the yard (health and safety again). The enthusiastic Ronnie went through his convincingly swift and balletic swordplay routine.

Sweet tooth? Visit Sue's confectionery with its rows of jars and boxes full of dainties you thought were extinct: Love Hearts, aniseed twists, acid drops, Pontefract cakes, rhubarb and custard bonbons and sherbet dips – they're all here. Sue weighs out the goodies on an appropriately old-style metal set of scales, and presents them in one of those twist-top paper bags.

The real Aladdin's Cave, though, is Tibbs' Collectables on the first floor. The impression is of a toyshop that

Tibbs' Collectables. (Graham Phythian)

blurs into a wealth of desirable bric-à-brac and curios. Besides the sheer quantity of stuff, it's the size of some items that grabs the attention: a doll's house as big as your fireplace, a thigh-high Paddington bear, and a gleaming yacht that you could imagine ruling the waves on Platt Fields Lake. There are model light aeroplanes that make you think that if hobbits were ever to take up crop-dusting, here is where they'd pick up their flying machines.

Throughout the Village, there was a general amused scepticism about the antiques programmes on TV. We all love the tales of an eggcup, bought for 50p at a car boot sale, that turns out to be a vodka cup presented by Fabergé to the Russian Tsar and therefore fetching a seven-figure sum. But how many of these tales are concocted or hyped for the sake of publicity or viewing figures? If you're interested, pop along to the Village: these people know their stuff.

DANGER MOUSE AND FRIENDS

Do you remember Captain Kremmen? He was Kenny Everett's alter ego, the lantern-jawed cartoon space cowboy with the gorgeous sidekick, Carla. Not blessed with a high IQ, but still the most fabulous man in the universe, the Captain would embark on adventures in his rocket ship Troll-1. These were mainly concerned with overcoming the evil Thargoids or the even worse Sun-Suckers. Forget Doctor Who and his two hearts, Captain Kremmen had bionic veins, as well as a detachable left big toe which converted into a space cannon.

Or how about Bananaman? By nature an awkward adolescent with a jokey north country accent, after downing a banana – an act reminiscent of Popeye and his spinach – our lad would turn with a flash and a shazam into a masked and V-shaped superhero with a six pack. Clad in his cloak and bright blue and yellow gear, he would now set about righting wrongs. In one episode his mission was to counter the machinations of the evil genius who had successfully plotted to – wait for it – cancel the midnight movie. Leaving aside for the moment why this should have been of concern to Bananaman's target audience, rest assured that in true superhero tradition the villain was always left gnashing his teeth.

Of course we all remember Danger Mouse, with his eyepatch and his bumbling assistant Penfold (guess whose nickname when he was a teacher). Sir David Jason and Terry Scott did the voices, and the arch villain Baron Silas Greenback, played by Edward Kelsey (Joe Grundy in *The Archers*), was the Blofeld to DM's Bond. The monocular mouse had his secret hideaway in a postbox on the corner of London's Baker Street: one of many nods to English culture. The puns were painfully English too: 'We are under a screw.' 'Oh, you mean you're under attack.'

Count Duckula (also voiced by David Jason) was former deadly enemy of Danger Mouse. During his latest reincarnation ritual, however, the blood was accidentally replaced with tomato ketchup. The result: the world's first vegetarian vampire duck.

As the reader will probably have worked out by now, this article is in memory of the late lamented Cosgrove Hall studios (1969-2009), which used to have their base on Albany Road, Chorlton. The list of TV animations that poured from the prolific Cosgrove Hall workshops is impressive: Doctor Who and Terry Pratchett spin-offs, Roald Dahl's BFG, *Postman Pat*, *Peter and the Wolf*, and *Fifi and the Flowertots*, to name but a few. New full-colour life was breathed into the monochrome children's classics of the 1950s: Bill and Ben, Andy Pandy, Noddy and Sooty all received the CH treatment, no doubt captivating a new generation of pre-school viewers.

The model-based animation that deservedly won a BAFTA and an Emmy was the delightful *The Wind in the Willows*. It was a fifty-two-episode television series in the mid-1980s, with a star-studded cast of voices: David Jason again, Sir Michael Hordern, the late Ian Carmichael (TV's definitive Bertie Wooster), Peter Sallis (Norman Clegg in *Last of the Summer Wine*), Daphne Oxenford (the voice of *Listen With Mother*), and the late Richard Pearson (Victor Meldrew's brother in *One Foot in the Grave*).

The world of Toad, Mole, Ratty and Badger was recreated with sets that showed microscopic attention to detail. The character models had minute ball and socket mechanisms inside them which made possible a convincingly wide range of expressions and movement.

Cosgrove Hall's *The Wind in the Willows* is a national treasure, as warming and nourishing as a full English breakfast, and the antithesis of the brash and in-your-face style of many modern animations. The pace is gentler and simpler, less hectic with competition and hidden agendas: a celebration of a vanished world.

ABOUT THE AUTHOR

GRAHAM PHYTHIAN writes a local history column for the *South Manchester Reporter* and is a regular contributor to *Soccer History* magazine. He is the author of five books on regional and sport history, including *Colossus: The True Story of William Foulke*. He lives in Chorlton, Manchester.

The Worrall scandal hits the headlines (see page 40): a *Manchester Evening News* vendor in the city centre. The cricket details confirm the date as August 1895. (Philip Lloyd)

If you enjoyed this book, then you may also be interested in . . .

Manchester: From the Robert Banks Collection
JAMES STANHOPE-BROWN

This collection of archive photographs, taken by professional photographer Robert Banks working in Manchester during the 1900s, offers a rare glimpse of some of the events that were taking place in the city at the time. Featuring snapshots of street scenes, whit walks, temperance marches, football matches and royal visits to the city, this book captures Manchester at the turn of the last century and is an essential volume for everyone with an interest in the history of the city.

978 0 7524 6013 0

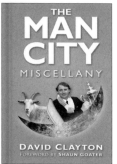

The Man City Miscellany
DAVID CLAYTON

The Man City Miscellany is packed with lists, statistics, tables, song lyrics, quotes and facts – such as the name of Clive Allen's dog, and the meaning behind the 'Invisible Man' the City fans sing about. From club record holders to bizarre goal celebrations, and from peculiar player nicknames to the ups and downs of City's chequered history, this is the only trivia book a Blues fan could ever need.

978 0 7524 6373 5

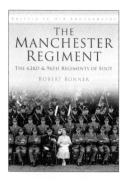

The Manchester Regiment: The 63rd & 96th of Foot
ROBERT BONNER

This illustrated regimental history features photographs from the 1860s and the last days of the Manchester Regiment in 1958, when it ceased to exist as a distinct unit. During this time the Regiment served in most parts of the Empire including areas as diverse as India, South Africa, Egypt, Palestine, Singapore, Malaya and, later, Germany. With 200 photographs from the Museum of the Manchester Regiment, this volume provides an fascinating pictorial insight into the history of the Regiment.

978 0 7524 6015 4

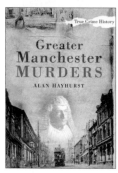

Greater Manchester Murders
ALAN HAYHURST

This book details some of the most notorious murders in the history of Greater Manchester. They include the case of cat burglar, Charlie Peace, who killed 20-year-old PC Nicholas Cook, and only confessed when he had already been sentenced to death for another murder; William Robert Taylor, whose young daughter was killed in a boiler explosion and who later murdered his three remaining children; and John Jackson, who escaped from Strangeways Gaol by killing a prison warder.

978 0 7509 5091 6

Visit our website and discover thousands of other History Press books.
www.thehistorypress.co.uk